Baja California

By the *Sunset* Editorial Staff with Ken and Caroline Bates

LANE BOOKS • MENLO PARK, CALIFORNIA

Acknowledgments

We wish to make special acknowledgment of the help given by many people in the preparation of this book. Among these people are Virginia and Cirilo Gomez of Santiago; Frank Fischer of San Ignacio; Harrison Evans of Mulegé; Thomas A. Robertson of San Miguel Village; Hector Arce of San Ignacio; William J. Morris of the geology department of Occidental College in Los Angeles; Joe Roynon; Bruce Berger; and Katie Lee.

Assistance also was given by Eliseo Garcia Araujo, Aurelio Ibarra Vega, and Enrique Sanchez Mayans of the Department of Tourism, State of Baja California; and Lic. Ricardo Garcia Soto and Lic. Cesar Aramburo Rosas of the Department of Tourism, Territory of Baja California Sur.

The editors of *Sunset Magazine*, who for many years have provided *Sunset* readers with feature articles on Baja California, provided special help in planning the book's editorial approach.

We are grateful for the help of special consultants George E. Lindsay, director of the California Academy of Sciences; Reid Moran, curator of botany at the Natural History Museum in San Diego; William Aplin; and Arnold Senterfitt.

Most of all, we wish to thank freelance writers Ken and Caroline Bates, who on assignment from Sunset's editors traveled thousands of miles through the rugged country of Baja California, compiling information and writing the basic manuscript. Most of the photographs in the book were taken by Ken, including the cover photograph of Coyote Bay on the west side of Concepción Bay. The aerial photo on page 12 is by Robert Cox, the lower photo on page 16 and the upper left photo on page 75 are by Glenn Christiansen, and the photos on page 18 and 25 are by Darrow M. Watt.

Edited by Phyllis Elving

Cartography: Roberta A. Dillow
Topographical Map: Art Technology
Design: Lawrence A. Laukhuf

Contents

An Introduction to

Baja California

Mexico's 800-mile-long peninsula—magnificent desert country nearly surrounded by the sea, offering both wilderness travel and resort life

IT'S SLOW GOING as you bounce along "Cardon Boulevard." This stretch on bumpy and dusty Highway 1 is below the dry lake of Laguna Chapala.

A LARGE PART of Baja California is essentially the same today as it was when the Spaniards arrived more than 400 years ago. The peninsula is big—about 800 air miles long from the border at Tijuana to land's end at Cabo San Lucas, and 55,000 square miles in area. But except for the built-up northern border, the tropical city of La Paz, and a few towns and fishing resorts along the shores of the Sea of Cortez, most of it is uninhabited and undeveloped.

For sheer magnificence, ruggedness, and variety of scenery, Baja California is matched by few places on the continent. Most of the peninsula is desert—plains strewn with granite boulders and black lava rock, impenetrable thickets of thorny shrubs, and forests of some of the largest and strangest desert plants on earth. Running down the middle of the northern part is a granitic mountain range, a wilderness of pine forests in the higher reaches and of palm canyons on the steep eastern scarps. The center of the peninsula is a vast area of cactus-covered lava flows dotted with cinder cones and dissected by spring-fed canyons, small oases where date palms and subtropical fruits grow.

What gives Baja California its special grandeur and softens the harsh contours of the terrain is the sea that surrounds it. On the west the Pacific breaks on beaches piled with driftage. The cliff-backed coast resembles that of southern California, but most of it is utterly deserted. On the east the clear, warm waters of the Gulf of California—the Sea of Cortez—lap gently on dazzling white sands along a deeply indented coast of turquoise bays and coves popular with skin-divers. The Cortez, one of the greatest saltwater fishing areas in the world, is a giant aquarium and submarine pasture supporting incredible numbers of fish, from tiny tropical species to thousand-pound game fish.

The peninsula is still sufficiently remote and unknown that to some Americans it's "Baja, California," a town vaguely placed somewhere on the outskirts of Los Angeles. Baja California means Lower California, a name the early Spanish settlers used to distinguish the peninsula from Alta (or Upper) California, as the present state of California was known. Baja California is politically divided into two units at the 28th parallel: The northern half is a state, the southern half a federal territory.

It is now easy to reach La Paz and the tropical towns of the Cortez by plane or ferry. But penetrating the primitive interior is an adventure even in a well-equipped vehicle. The network of roads connecting the small settlements and isolated ranches is an obstacle course of rocks, ruts, and dusty chuckholes. A few have been "improved." Many, however, are scarcely better (and some are worse) than the original Camino Real hacked through the desert jungle by the early Spanish missionaries. For many people, the absence of asphalt highways has much to do with Baja's appeal. As the naturalist Joseph Wood Krutch wrote, "Baja is a splendid example of what bad roads can do for a country. It must be almost as beautiful as it was when the first white man saw it in 1533."

THE EARLY COLONIZERS

Nearly a century before the Pilgrims landed at Plymouth, Hernán Cortés' conquistadors sailed into La Paz Bay in search of treasure. Though Cortés himself established a settlement at La Paz in 1535, it lasted for only about two years, and for the next 150 years all Spanish attempts to establish a colonial outpost in Baja California failed. They found pearls in the Sea of Cortez, but the harsh, arid land defeated them. It wasn't until the Jesuits, under the leadership of Father Juan María Salvatierra,

DIRT ROADS of Baja can be a challenge, but for many they are part of the peninsula's appeal.

founded Loreto in 1697 that the first successful colonization of the peninsula began. .

From Loreto, the political and religious capital of Baja for more than a century, the Jesuits explored much of the peninsula, establishing 20 mission settlements and a network of connecting trails. The Jesuits were the peninsula's first farmers, planting grain, grapes, olives, dates, and figs.

The Indians gathered into the mission settlements were nomadic peoples who wandered with the seasons, hunting, fishing, gathering wild plants. Epidemics of smallpox, typhus, and syphilis—diseases introduced by the Spaniards—swept through the settlements and decimated the Indians. The original Indian population of the peninsula has been variously estimated between 25,000 and 75,000. Now only about 500 remain in northern Baja.

In 1767, political machinations in the Spanish court resulted in the ouster of the Jesuits from Baja. They were replaced by the Franciscans, under Father Junípero Serra, who during their five-year tenure founded only the mission of San Fernando. The Franciscans went on to more fertile pastures of Alta California. The Dominicans, the last missionaries in Baja, established nine more missions and replaced some of the adobe churches of the Jesuits with stone structures. Of the 30 missions founded in Baja, only a few constructed of solid stone have survived.

HOW TO GET THERE

There are four border crossings between Baja California and the United States. Tijuana and Mexicali are open 24 hours a day. Tecate and Algodones are open from 8 a.m. to midnight.

Two airlines have jet service between the United States and Baja. Aeronaves de Mexico makes flights from Los Angeles to La Paz and Tijuana; Air West has flights between Tucson and La Paz. Aeronaves del Norte flies twin-engine planes between Guaymas and Tijuana with stops at Santa Rosalía, Guerrero Negro, San Felipe, and Mexicali; Aeronaves del Oeste twin-engine planes fly between Guaymas and La Paz via Santa Rosalía, Mulegé, and Loreto and between Mazatlán and La Paz via Los Mochis and Villa Constitución. Aerolíneas del Pacífico makes daily flights between Los Mochis and La Paz. Servicios Aereos operates an air-taxi service between La Paz and Cape region resorts.

Three ferries operate between the Mexican mainland and Baja California. All carry automobiles and trucks. Two run between Mazatlán and La Paz, the other from Topolobampo to La Paz. An automobile ferry will eventually run from Guaymas to Santa Rosalía and down the coast to La Paz, stopping en route at Puerto Escondido; it will re-

UNDER WATCHFUL EYE of customs, pleasure boat ties up in Santa Rosalía harbor.

turn by the same route. This ferry was expected to go into operation by the end of 1971. Initially, its route will be limited to the trip between Guaymas and Santa Rosalía.

The Sonora-Baja California Railway runs between Mexicali and Mexico City. A number of different private bus lines operate between Tijuana and Mexicali, Mexicali and San Felipe, Tijuana and Ensenada, Tecate and Ensenada, and south of Ensenada as far as El Rosario. Private lines in La Paz serve the Cape region and Santo Domingo.

Driving in Baja

The vehicles most suitable for driving Baja California's dirt roads are pickup trucks with four-speed transmissions, four-wheel-drive vehicles, dune buggies, and motorcycles. A few passenger cars negotiate the roads, but they are not recommended. Deep chuckholes, dips, and ruts require high-clearance vehicles.

The most important advice for anyone driving the peninsula for the first time is *drive slowly*. Don't overload. This is one of the most common causes of breakdown. If possible, make the trip in the company of at least one other vehicle, particularly if exploring infrequently traveled side roads.

Gas in border towns costs about 30 cents a gallon and up, depending upon the octane rating. Farther down the peninsula, gas sold from drums costs 40 to 55 cents a gallon. Carry a large chamois to filter any dirt or water that may be in gas bought from drums.

Equipping your vehicle. A skid plate should be installed under the oil pan if the vehicle is not so equipped. (Also consider installing one under the gas tank if it is vulnerable.) Heavy-duty shocks, helper springs, or extra leaves in springs may be necessary, depending upon the clearance of the vehicle and the load to be carried.

Tires should be in good condition and have strong sidewalls and a thick tread. Special tires are not necessary for driving the main peninsular highway to La Paz or the principal side roads, but carry two or three spares. On dirt roads let the air out until the tires flex over rocks (20 to 22 pounds).

Flotation tires offer some advantages. They don't sink as deeply in sand and mud, and they absorb some of the shock of rough surfaces. However, flotation tires add little or nothing to road clearance and have several drawbacks. Special wheels are required, sometimes also the cutting out of fenders. The tires are more expensive, and only a few dealers stock them.

Both standard and flotation tires may be either tube-type or tubeless. The ease with which a flat can be fixed is an important consideration. Since compressed air is not available throughout most of the peninsula, take along some inner tubes if you use tubeless tires.

Flats caused in tubeless tires by cactus can be stopped by jacking up the wheel, removing the tire valve (with the tire still mounted), and pouring in a puncture sealer. This is a simple way to repair "cactus flats," but it coats the inside of the tire and makes it difficult to patch or to use later with an inner tube.

Take two jacks, one a three-ton hydraulic, the other a high-lift bumper jack. You should have several spare inner tubes and everything necessary to repair a tire, including a tube liner, plugs, patches, adhesive, tire pump, and a bead breaker. Also take a tow rope (at least 6,000 pounds test) and a short-handled spade or military trencher. For extra gas carry at least two five-gallon jerry cans. Special mounting devices make it possible to mount the cans inside or outside the vehicle.

A mail order catalogue of equipment used for traveling on the peninsula is available from Dick Cepek, a dealer who specializes in selling flotation tires and wheels as well as many Baja accessories. His address is 9201 California Avenue, South Gate, California 90280. The catalogue is free.

Automobile permits. An automobile permit is not required for travel on the Baja peninsula. It is required on the Mexican mainland, so you must obtain one to take your car across the Gulf on a ferry. Permits are free and are good for six months. They may be obtained at Mexican customs at any point of entry into Baja or at the Mexican customs

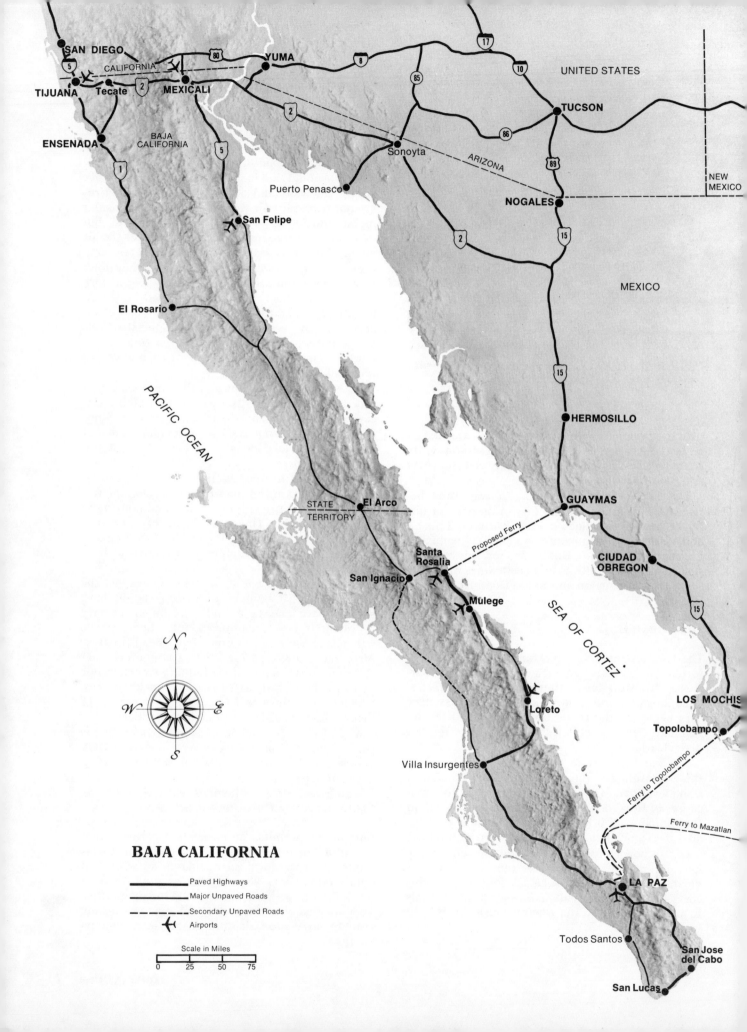

BAJA CALIFORNIA

—————— Paved Highways
—————— Major Unpaved Roads
– – – – – Secondary Unpaved Roads
✈ Airports

Scale in Miles

0   25   50   75

office in La Paz. Proof of ownership is required. If you do not own the vehicle, you will need a notarized statement from the owner as well as the ownership papers.

Insurance. Your U.S. automobile (or boat or aircraft) insurance will not cover you in Baja. Although insurance is not required, some coverage is desirable. Mexican insurance companies are government regulated and offer the same terms and rates. Insurance can be started the day you cross the border and stopped the day you return. Many brokers (including auto clubs) say that short-term policies for travel in Mexico are not profitable and set minimums on the coverage they sell. Agents at border towns usually have no minimums.

Contrary to popular belief, Mexican insurance will not keep you out of jail. A traffic accident is a criminal offense in Mexico. In a traffic accident where there is any show of blood, all drivers and vehicles must be held until an investigation can be made by the district attorney. Even in a minor accident, you may be held until liability has been determined, fines and damages paid.

Trailers. Trailers are treated like automobiles, and special permits are not required unless the units are more than 40 feet long and 8 feet wide. They may be left on rented or leased property, but only for the period of time extended to the visitor on his tourist card. Trailers cannot safely go below Puertecitos on the Gulf, El Rosario on the Pacific.

Small-boat cruising

To bring a fishing or pleasure boat 17 feet or longer into Baja, you must post a cash bond with Mexican customs at the port of entry. The bond, which is 1% of the importation fee on the boat, usually is between $20 and $40. Bring your ownership and registration papers. The bond will be returned when the boat is removed from Mexico. Boats may be left on the peninsula for the duration of your tourist permit. No permit or bond is required for boats under 17 feet.

The poor condition of the roads prohibits trailering a boat below Puertecitos on the Gulf and El Rosario on the Pacific. There are concrete ramps at San Felipe and Puertecitos and many beaches along this coast where a boat can be launched.

The recommended course for cruising down the Cortez is described in Sunset's *The Sea of Cortez*.

Flying a private plane

To depart the United States and enter Mexico by private plane you will need an outbound flight plan with the FAA, a tourist card for each passenger, and proof of plane ownership and registration. Mexican insurance is recommended. Your first landing in Baja must be at Tijuana, Mexicali, or La Paz. At the airport of entry you file a flight plan, obtain a General Declaration permit for the plane, and pay a radio use fee of about $1.46 to RAMSA. (Radio Aeronautica Mexicana, S.A., RAMSA for short, provides aeronautical radio navigation and communication service, weather information, flight plan service.)

Clear through Tijuana or Mexicali again when you leave Baja. You must depart with the same passengers that entered—unless you have permission to do otherwise. Returning to the United States, you must land first at a U.S. airport of entry for customs and immigration inspection. Advise the FAA Flight Service Station of your flight plan at least 30 minutes in advance of arrival.

CROSSING THE BORDER

Tourist cards are not required in Baja's border area (as far south as Maneadero on the Pacific and San Felipe on the Gulf) if you stay 72 hours or less. However, anyone traveling below this area or planning to stay longer than 72 hours must have one.

Tourist cards are free and are of two types: the single-entry card (no photographs required) and the multiple-entry card (three passport-type photographs required). Both are good for 6 months, the maximum length of time you may stay in Baja. A birth certificate or other proof of citizenship is necessary to obtain a tourist card. The cards are issued at the border, at Mexican consulates, and at Mexican Government tourist offices.

To take a pet into Baja you need a certificate stating that the animal is "free from symptoms of contagious or infectious disease." Dogs require anti-rabies inoculation. The certificate must be signed by a licensed veterinarian and countersigned and stamped by the U.S. Department of Agriculture in your state. Have it visaed ($4) by the Mexican consul nearest to where you live.

Mexican customs regulations

Clothing and other personal belongings such as jewelry, luggage, books, sporting goods, and camping equipment may be brought into Mexico duty free. Each tourist is permitted to bring in one still camera, one movie camera, and 12 rolls of film for each.

Mexico has strict regulations on what may be exported from the country. Indian artifacts and petrified wood are on the prohibited list.

U.S. customs regulations

Residents of the United States can bring back from Baja $100 worth of articles (retail value) duty free every 31 days. No minimum stay is required to earn this exemption. Be sure to keep receipts for items bought in Mexico. The $100 exemption may not be applied to merchandise you ship to your home.

You may send gifts of not more than $10 (retail value) duty free to persons in the United States, providing the same person does not receive more than $10 worth of gifts in one day. Such gifts do not have to be declared when you cross the border and do not come under your $100 exemption. Write "Gift Enclosed—Value Under $10" on the package.

Before crossing the border into Baja, register all trademarked or foreign-made articles of value (such as cameras and binoculars) at U.S. customs.

If you return to the United States through California, you may not bring in any alcoholic beverages by private car, plane, or boat, unless you possess a state liquor importer's license or are a non-resident passing through the state. If you come on a "common carrier," you may bring one quart of wine or liquor. If you enter via Arizona, you may bring in one quart by private conveyance.

WHERE TO STAY

While Baja's resorts are not exactly havens for the budget vacationer, they do offer a range of prices. (The really inexpensive accommodations are limited to a few native guesthouses and hotels.) Near the border, motels cater to the motorist and charge north-of-the-border prices. Farther down the peninsula, resorts depend upon fly-in sportsmen. A warm tropical sun, the blue Sea of Cortez, and white sandy beaches are the natural attributes shared by all these fly-in resorts. The price you pay to enjoy such surroundings depends on whether you stay in a cabana of palm-thatch simplicity or a sea-view suite of great luxury.

Most of these resorts originally owed their existence to the fly-in sportfisherman. All outside La Paz have their own airstrips and fishing fleets. A decade ago they were patronized principally by fishermen. Now it is estimated that forty per cent of the guests don't fish at all. They play tennis, ride horseback, swim in resort pools, skin-dive.

Almost all the resorts, including many hotels in La Paz, offer accommodations only on the American plan. (Through travelers can stop for lunch or dinner at all the Cape region resorts and many on the Gulf coast.) The food served is a mixture of "American," "continental," and familiar Mexican dishes, generally with less emphasis on the native cuisine. Fresh seafood is featured.

Reservations at all resorts should be made well in advance of major holidays. Deposits must accompany reservations, and you usually have to give one or two week's notice prior to your arrival date to obtain a refund.

Tipping is not expected in Baja, except on sportfishing boats or where special services are rendered. Some resorts request guests not to tip. Instead, they add a surcharge (about 10%) to the bill.

Pilots, and others, can make room and boat reservations at any resort through Patricia Senterfitt, Pilot Reservation Service, Tierra Ranch, Lakeside, California 92040; phone number is (714) 442-0927.

CAMPING

A pickup truck with a camper shell is the ideal setup for Baja travel but is not a necessity. Most of the peninsula is wild, unfenced desert, and putting up a tent or unrolling a sleeping bag is simply a matter of picking the site of your choice.

In Baja garbage disposal is a problem for campers. There are no garbage cans or collectors in the wild desert, and nowhere is the lack more apparent than on the northern Gulf shores and at popular camping sites on Concepción Bay. Actual food scraps should be scattered on the desert, not buried with cans and bottles. Animals and birds will quickly eat everything that's edible. Cans should be burned (tops and bottoms removed), flattened, and buried. If not burned, coyotes attracted by the scent of food will dig them up.

Anyone driving the central desert should carry a supply of canned goods. Even if you plan to eat at ranches en route, a few canned foods will get you through should your vehicle break down. Grocery stores (abarrotes) are far between in the central desert. You'll find canned goods and supplies at El Rosario, San Felipe, El Arco, San Ignacio, Santa Rosalía, Mulegé, Loreto, and Villa Constitución. Off the main highway, there are well-stocked stores at Guerrero Negro and a few supplies at Los Angeles Bay. Ice is generally not available.

Carry a good supply of water. Allow a gallon per person per day, and always keep several days' supply. If you can, take enough for the entire trip.

Bring enough stove fuel to last the entire trip— it is not sold on the peninsula except at border towns. Aviation gas can be used as a substitute fuel in stoves but not in lanterns. However, it will blacken pots.

Baja is the home of 10 species of rattlesnakes. They are most active during spring months after dark. Some precautions should be taken when gathering firewood. Mexican wood gatherers often toss rocks into brush to detect their presence. Be careful picking up firewood—a favorite hiding place of scorpions. Shake out any bedding, clothes, and shoes left outdoors at night.

Camping on the desert, you are bound to run afoul of several vicious types of cholla cacti. The jointed variety has arms that grow in short segments and fall, littering the ground. One variety is known as the "jumping cholla." If a trouser leg or shoelace brushes against one of the spines, the cholla snags the cloth, swings around your leg as you walk, and jabs deeply into the flesh. You need a pair of pliers to remove it.

HUNTING AND FISHING

There is good hunting for mule deer and desert black-tailed jackrabbit, abundant throughout the peninsula. Special permits are required to hunt mountain lion and the rare bighorn sheep. (Bighorn permits cost $400 to $800, and only about 50 are issued annually.) The principal game birds are California and Gambel's quail, mourning and white-winged dove, and a variety of wintering ducks and geese (including black brant, which frequent salt-

 DISTINCTIVE PLANTS OF BAJA

"Poor shrubs, useless thorn bushes, and bare rocks," wrote one discouraged missionary of the deserts of Baja. Later travelers found this land to contain one of the most curious collections of desert shrubs and thorn bushes in the world. While many of Baja's desert species—palo verdes, mesquites, and creosote bushes, for example—are recognizable to anyone familiar with southern Arizona, others are strange and even unique.

Oddest-looking is the *cirio*, or boojum (*Idria columnaris*) a polelike tree that makes the north-central desert a landscape of surreal shapes. Tallest is the cardon, *Pachycereus pringlei*, a massive cactus with upsweeping arms that resembles the saguaro of Arizona. In March and April, the fluted branches are clustered with white flowers, followed by fuzzy tan fruits filled with black seeds. Inside the trunk is a skeleton of hardwood rods used for house walls and rafters, fences, and bedsprings.

There are several varieties of yucca. *Yucca valida*, a tree yucca natives call *datilla* or *datilillo*, is the largest, with thick, swordlike leaves and clusters of creamy flowers in summer.

The thick-trunked elephant tree *(Pachycormus discolor)* of the central desert has a tawny bark that peels off like paper. The tree appears lifeless most of the year, but rains bring out tiny compound leaves along the contorted branches. In June and July it sends forth sprays of pink or whitish yellow flowers. Two other thick-trunked trees, *torote* and *copal* (both of the genus Bursera), are also called "elephant trees." After shedding their leaves the three can be difficult to tell apart. However, *Pachycormus discolor* has no aroma. If you break off a twig from one of the other two, a pungent piney scent stays on your fingers for hours.

Sweet and sour pitahayas, *pitahaya dulce* and *pitahaya agría*, produce highly prized fruits. The

sweet pitahaya *(Lemaireocereus thurberi)*—the organ pipe cactus of southwestern Arizona—is abundant from about El Arco south. Waxy, pink-tinged white flowers appear in late May and June. Spiny crimson fruits, about the size of golf balls, ripen in midsummer. They taste like a cross between watermelon and strawberry. The sour pitahaya *(Machaerocereus gummosus)*, a spiny, sprawling cactus with dark green or dirty gray branches, grows almost everywhere in the peninsula. The fruits have a citruslike flavor.

Many chollas grow in Baja, and all are armed with fierce spines. Several species have segmented branches that fall to the ground and "spring" on any passerby.

The northern, wandlike ocotillo grows as far south as Mulegé. The bushy, branching southern ocotillo, known as *palo adán*—"Adam's tree"—because it is naked of leaves most of the year, starts north of Los Angeles Bay. Both bear tubular scarlet flowers at the tips of the branches.

A strange cactus called the creeping devil (the Mexicans call it *chirinola*) is found only on the Magdalena Plain around Santo Domingo. The thick, sharp-spined branches creep along the ground, rooting on the undersides, and as they inch forward the oldest extremity dies.

Agaves are represented in Baja by several species. A single towering stalk rises from each rosette of succulent, needle-tipped leaves and terminates in a mass of brilliant yellow blossoms in April and May. After one flowering, the plant dies.

Three common trees in southern Baja are the wild fig tree *(zalate)*, whose tortuous white roots crawl over boulders; the tall, graceful palo blanco, with a silvery trunk and whitish yellow acacialike flowers that bloom in March and April; and a native "plum" with large, spreading limbs which grows wild south of La Paz and bears tiny, rather tasteless red or yellow fruits.

LANDING STRIP and sport-fishing pier are short walk from Serenidad resort at Rio Mulegé.

Fishing

The only requirement for fishing in Baja is a license, easy to obtain from border authorities, port captains, or fishing resorts. Fees are 48 cents for three days, 96 cents for a month, $2 for three months, and $4 for a year. Ask about seasons and limits when you obtain your license.

All fish brought over the border must be declared. The United States permits you to bring back 35 pounds of small fish or one large fish. (The fish may be cleaned, but heads and tails must be intact.)

Shellfishing laws are becoming more restrictive. The taking of lobster and abalone is illegal everywhere on the peninsula; only duly licensed commercial fish cooperatives can catch these shellfish. To have a lobster in your possession, you must have an invoice (receipt) showing that it was bought through a cooperative or authorized fish dealer. With such a receipt, you may take lobster out of the country. But be sure to ask the fish dealer how many lobsters can be purchased and taken over the border, because this varies with each season.

WATER SPORTS

Baja has hundreds of miles of unspoiled beaches. The Gulf Coast has no surf, but on the Pacific, where there are few offshore islands, many surfing spots have waves equal to the best in Southern California. At present most surfing is done between the California border and Ensenada.

Twelve varieties of stingrays and 30 kinds of sharks live in Baja waters. Wear an old pair of shoes to protect your feet when you go in swimming, because rays bury into the sand in shallow water. A little underwater noise, such as rapping two stones together, will scare them away.

There are dive shops at Ensenada, La Paz, and Punta Banda. Scuba gear can be obtained at resorts in Mulegé and Loreto. The hotel at Punta Chivato is well equipped with at least 12 complete outfits including tanks, weights, regulating valves, and spear guns. Scuba equipment is also available on the South Cape, where a full-time instructor shuttles between resorts. Regularly scheduled skin-diving excursions originate from La Paz.

OTHER TRAVEL INFORMATION

When you travel to Baja California from the United States you are traveling to another country, with its own language, laws, standards, and way of life. Furthermore, much of Baja is a remote wilderness, creating more differences. Familiarize yourself with special precautions that may be advisable.

water bays on the Pacific and in the Cape).

The Sea of Cortez has been described as the world's best fishing hole, and 650 species of fish have been identified in the upper 200 fathoms. Half are rated as game fish.

Hunting

You can obtain a hunting permit from the office of the Secretaria de Agricultura y Ganaderia—Delegación Forestal y Caza, in Tijuana or Mexicali. You must apply for this permit before taking your guns across the border. The permit costs $19.20 and is valid for six months. For information and assistance in obtaining a permit, contact the office of the Mexican Government Tourism Department in Tijuana, Mexicali, Los Angeles, or San Diego. Ask for a list of open and closed seasons when you obtain your hunting license. Seasons and bag limits vary from year to year.

You may take a gun into Baja but only for the purpose of sport hunting. To do so you will need a consular certificate and a military certificate in addition to a hunting license. Any Mexican consulate can explain the regulations.

Health conditions

The food and water problems associated with cities on mainland Mexico don't exist on much of the Baja California peninsula, where there are few populated areas. However, tap water is not safe to drink in most of the larger communities, and bottled water should be used where available. Some grocery stores sell spring and distilled water from the United States in gallon plastic containers. The water used by the better restaurants and hotels comes in five-gallon glass bottles. Bottled locally, it is obtained from deep wells and springs.

Elsewhere the problem is less one of good water than of any water at all. In the arid and sparsely settled central desert, the existence of a ranch or village depends on a water supply, usually safe but occasionally questionable. In many towns in the Territory—Mulegé, Loreto, San Miguel Comondú, and settlements south of La Paz—you'll see concrete water faucets, in the shape of geometric S's, near the center of town. On the outskirts you may pass an "SSA Bombeo" plant, the water-pumping station. The initials SSA stand for health. While the government enforces no minimum water quality standards, it has advised each village on the fundamentals of a good water supply. The water usually is safe to drink.

There is no reason to avoid fruits and vegetables that can't be peeled. Most of the peninsula crops (including thin-skinned tomatoes) are flown or trucked to California and sold in the largest supermarket chains. The precautions you take at home —washing fresh produce thoroughly in water— apply in Baja as well.

Pasteurized and homogenized milk is available in the larger northern towns, Guerrero Negro, Santa Rosalía, and La Paz. Raw milk should be avoided. Fresh cheeses, such as goat's milk cheese, are very risky.

A smallpox vaccination is no longer required. Tetanus and typhoid shots are not mandatory but are a wise precaution, and anyone camping in Baja should have them. Other immunization is not needed.

Communications

Tijuana, Mexicali, Tecate, Ensenada, and La Paz have telephone service to the United States. Service to and from the first four is normally good, but telephoning from La Paz may take time. A municipal telephone line continues down the coast from Ensenada to El Rosario, linking towns along the way. A similar line connects the towns of the Cape region with La Paz. Collect calls can't be made.

At a few resorts it is possible to call the United States via the high seas radiotelephone system. Another method used to communicate with the United States is amateur radio. From the United States you can telephone ham radio operators in either the United States or Mexico who may be able to contact Baja resorts that have amateur stations and plug you in.

Almost every community of any size on the peninsula has a telegraph office. It usually takes two days for a telegram to reach the United States. Always include your address in the *body* of the telegram, because it may be cut off the end.

Tijuana, Mexicali, Santa Rosalía, Loreto, and La Paz have direct air mail service. Other communities have some form of mail service, but in small villages the mail may be carried out by private individuals.

Money

Hotels, restaurants, and stores in the larger communities as well as remote ranches that sell gas and soft drinks accept U.S. money. Prices are often quoted in dollars, and many places seem to prefer American currency. It is a good idea to carry small denominations if traveling in isolated areas.

Personal checks are accepted only at resorts where you are known. Banks will cash travelers' checks, but other checks — including cashiers' checks and U.S. postal money orders — may raise difficulties. Good identification is essential. A passport with multiple photographs is useful for just this purpose. Except in the border towns and La Paz, credit cards are not accepted.

The official rate of exchange is 12.50 pesos for one U.S. dollar. The peso equals 8 cents U.S. currency, and there are 100 centavos in a peso.

Language

In Baja you'll find many Mexicans who speak English, but they won't all be in businesses that serve the tourist. For example, in La Paz (where the economy is dependent upon tourism) you probably won't find anyone in the post office, telephone company, telegraph office, or ferry office who admits he speaks or understands English. In small villages and remote areas, there may be one resident who comprehends what the *norteamericano* is trying to say, but he will be an exception.

A pocket-sized Spanish dictionary will help you cross the language barrier. Be sure to buy a dictionary with Spanish-American rather than Castilian pronunciations and with definitions that reflect Mexican or Latin-American usage. Also valuable is the Cuthbertson Verb Wheel.

Exploring the

North Region

*Lively towns near the border...
rugged mountains in the
interior...surf-swept Pacific
beaches and clear, warm Gulf waters*

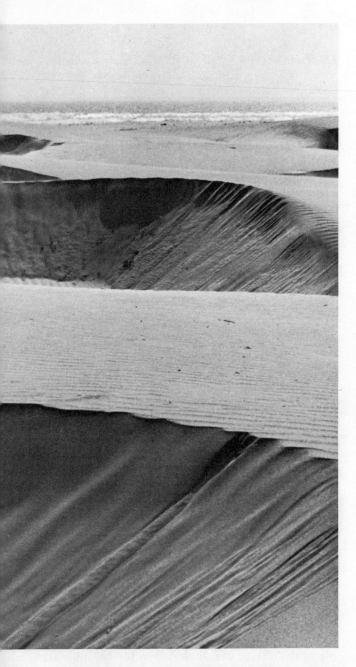

PACIFIC SHORE gets wilder and emptier as you travel south. These drifting dunes on broad beach near San Quintin Bay lie beyond pavement's end.

THE EASY accessibility and varied attractions of the first 200 miles of Baja's 800-mile-long peninsula make this area especially appealing to many travelers. Paved roads bring much of the peninsula's northern region within a few hours' drive of the United States. Close to the border are the large, lively towns that often provide people with their first taste of Mexico. The shops crammed with native crafts and folk art, the exciting jai alai games and bullfights are all familiar tourist attractions. Behind the tourist façade you can find the colorful life of Mexico, as warm and vibrant as the chiles that flavor the food.

Below the border the countryside looks much like California of fifty years ago. On the Pacific coast the surf-swept beaches are backed by hills dotted with farms and cattle ranches. The mountainous interior, a granitic fault block like the Sierra Nevada, is a near wilderness of cool pine forests, wildflower meadows, and snow-covered peaks—some more than 10,000 feet high. On the Gulf side the fertile farmland of the Mexicali Valley, an extension of the Imperial Valley to the north, is irrigated by the waters of the Colorado River.

There are also similarities in climate, although northern Baja, being farther south, is somewhat warmer. Early morning fogs and ocean breezes keep the Pacific coast cool in summer, and winter daytime temperatures hover in the 50's and 60's. A mantle of snow one to several feet deep may cover the high country in the winter months. In the Gulf deserts, winters are mild—and summers a scorching 115 to 120 degrees.

THE BORDER

Thousands of people every day pass beneath the great steel-and-concrete arch that connects the United States with Mexico at Tijuana, busiest of the four U.S. ports of entry to Baja California. Some are vacationers bound for Ensenada or Baja's remote camping, hunting, and fishing grounds. Many are commuters. Quite a few are one-day visitors, attracted by Tijuana's lively night life and sporting events or its dazzling shopping bazaar. Californians—San Diegans in particular—use the city almost like a suburb, border-hopping

TIJUANA AFTER DARK comes alive with neons and night people. Many gift shops stay open late.

STROLLING MARIACHIS serenade you with Mexican songs in Tijuana's many restaurants.

freely. For racing fans Tijuana is Agua Caliente, where the dogs or horses are running. For office girls the city is a bargain basement for perfumes, cosmetics, clothing, and beauty salons.

A relaxing of customs regulations makes it easy to border-hop: No tourist card is required if you stay less than 72 hours and don't travel below Maneadero on the Pacific or San Felipe on the Gulf.

Tijuana

There are several Tijuanas. Best known is "border-town" Tijuana with its racetrack, bullrings, and some 300 colorful curio stores lining Revolución Avenue and overflowing onto side streets. There is nothing quite like the tide of humanity thronging Revolución on Saturday night, a fascinating cultural mix of Mexicans and Americans of all ages and from every walk of life. Nor does any other street promise so much: a glitter of neons advertising psychedelic bars, topless floor shows, and fast action for marriages and divorces.

Tijuana is also a large city with a life apart from the tourist trade, one which most visitors never see or glimpse only briefly. Off the tourist track are native shops and markets (the main shopping area is along Constitución Avenue); food vendors with barrows of fruits, hot tacos, and ices and drinks; and sidewalk cubbyholes aromatic with tamales, bowls of steaming *menudo,* and spit-roasted chickens. On weekends there are band concerts and other entertainment, impromptu and planned, at the tree-shaded park of Teniente Guerrero, six blocks west of Revolución between Third and Fourth streets. Tijuana is also a city of 25 churches, several of which are impressive. One outstanding for its contemporary styling is Espíritu Santo on a hilltop near the Country Club.

A new Tijuana, with an image entirely different from the old, is rising on the shores of the Pacific just below the international border. At the center of the development is Playas de Tijuana, a modern residential beachfront community of houses and apartments. Nearby is Plaza Monumental, the "Bullring-by-the-Sea," and the long public beach. Cultural center of the area is Cortijo San José, which opened in 1970.

Cortijo San José. Described by its originators as a "Mexican fiesta village," the Cortijo combines the flavor of a working cattle ranch with the cultural pleasures of city life. Included in the complex are 14 shops built around a huge frescoed plaza, four restaurants, a theater, a convention hall and ballroom, and a ring for *charreadas*—Mexican-style rodeos—and bullfights. Only 6 miles from downtown Tijuana, Cortijo San José is reached via Calle

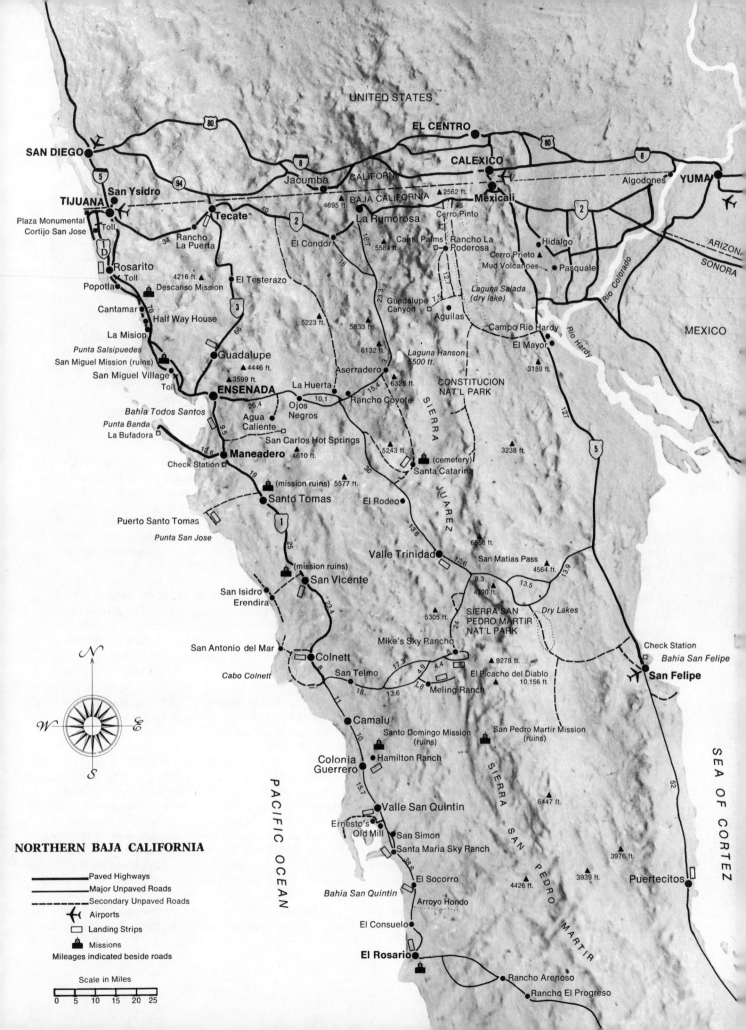

NORTHERN BAJA CALIFORNIA

UNITED STATES

SAN DIEGO

EL CENTRO

CALEXICO

Jacumba   CALIFORNIA

YUMA

Algodones

TIJUANA   **San Ysidro**

Tecate

BAJA CALIFORNIA

▲2562 ft.

Mexicali

Cerro Pinto

ARIZONA

SONORA

Plaza Monumental
Cortijo San Jose   Toll

La Rumorosa

4695 ft.   46

Rancho
La Puerta

El Condor

Cantu Palms   Rancho La
Poderosa

Hidalgo

MEXICO

Rosarito   Toll

4216 ft. ▲

El Testerazo

5584 ft.

Cerro Prieto

Mud Volcanoes

Pasquale

Popotla

Descanso Mission

16.7

Rio Colorado

Cantamar

*Laguna Salada
(dry lake)*

Half Way House

23.3

Guadalupe
Canyon

1.5

Aguilas

Campo Rio Hardy

La Mision

5223 ft.

5833 ▲

El Mayor

Punta Salsipuedes

San Miguel Mission (ruins)

Guadalupe

▲4446 ft.

6132 ft.

*Laguna Hanson
5500 ft.*

3159 ft.

Rio Hardy

San Miguel Village

▲3599 ft.

Aserradero

Toll

ENSENADA

La Huerta

6325 ft.

**CONSTITUCION
NAT'L PARK**

26.4

15.4

Bahia Todos Santos

10.1

Rancho Coyote

Ojos
Negros

Punta Banda

9.5

Agua
Caliente

SIERRA

La Bufadora

San Carlos Hot Springs

5243 ▲ ft.

3238 ft.

13.6

Maneadero

4610 ft.

(cemetery)

JUAREZ

Check Station

30

Santa Catarina

19

(mission ruins)   5577 ft.

Santo Tomas

El Rodeo

Puerto Santo Tomas

1

13.6

Punta San Jose

25

6658 ft.

Valle Trinidad

San Matias Pass

12.6

(mission ruins)

4564 ft.   13.9

San Vicente

8.3

San Isidro
Erendira

23.4

4390 ft.   13.5

5305 ft.

**SIERRA SAN
PEDRO MARTIR
NAT'L PARK**

Dry Lakes

24

Check Station

San Antonio del Mar

Mike's Sky Rancho

8

Bahia San Felipe

Colnett

17.3   4.9   4.4

9278 ft.

Cabo Colnett

8   San Telmo

1.8

El Picacho del Diablo
10,156 ft.

San Felipe

18   13.6

Meling Ranch

11

Camalu

Santo Domingo Mission
(ruins)

San Pedro Martir Mission
(ruins)

10

**Colonia
Guerrero**

Hamilton Ranch

6447 ft.

15.7

SIERRA

Valle San Quintin

Ernesto's
Old Mill

San Simon

SAN

San Simon

Santa Maria Sky Ranch

3976 ft.

38.6

PEDRO

Puertecitos

El Socorro

3939 ft.

Bahia San Quintin

4426 ft.

52

Arroyo Hondo

MARTIR

El Consuelo

El Rosario

Rancho Arenoso

Rancho El Progreso

SEA OF CORTEZ

PACIFIC OCEAN

NORTHERN BAJA CALIFORNIA

	Paved Highways
	Major Unpaved Roads
	Secondary Unpaved Roads
✈	Airports
▭	Landing Strips
⛪	Missions

Mileages indicated beside roads

Scale in Miles

0   5   10   15   20   25

N
W   E
S

BRASS BAND *plays as bullfight participants enter Cortijo San Jose ring. The Cortijo complex also includes gift shops, a theater-in-the-round, restaurants, and a convention hall and ballroom.*

Segunda and the toll highway 1D to Ensenada. Exit at Playas de Tijuana before the first tollhouse.

The style of the Cortijo is contemporary, the spirit traditional. The outside wall encircling it is symbolic of Mexico's rich heritage. Called "The Wall of Three Cultures," it blends modern bricks, Aztec stones excavated from ruins beneath Mexico City, and 400-year-old Spanish concrete. Also reflecting the melting-pot of cultures are the gift shops, where the work of artists and craftsmen from all over Mexico is displayed. The theater-in-the-round, which seats 600, emphasizes experimental works and will eventually become a school and center for the performing arts.

The entertainment is lively and traditionally Mexican. On weekend afternoons, starting around 2 p.m., *charreadas* are performed in the large roofed ring. Costumed *charros* and their feminine counterparts, *charras*, display riding skills and demonstrate tricky rope work. The exhibition is comparable to a rodeo, but with more style and verve. The admission charge is $2 for adults, $1 for children six to twelve; children under six are admitted free. Starting around noon, you can sit at tables arranged on ascending tiers around the ring and watch the warm-up activities. The only admission charge is the price of a bottle of beer. The free entertainment includes mock bullfights called *chaloteadas*. The bulls are not killed.

The clowning toreros are actually serious students of the bullfighting art. During the week Cortijo San José is a bullfighting school (many of

the students are girls), and anyone can take a lesson. The instructor, a professional matador, believes that a student can learn enough in 30 minutes to make a few passes with a live bull. The 30-minute lesson costs $5, after which you'll be allowed to enter the ring. *El toro* will be a heifer about a year and a half old. More serious students can take 10 lessons for $25.

Shopping. Tijuana, like the rest of Baja, is a free-trade zone where some imported products are sold duty-free. However, real savings attributable to this free-port status may be hard to find. Products made in the United States generally cost more in Tijuana, and the variety and quality of foreign imports is limited.

Tijuana stores overflow with Mexican arts and crafts. The best buys are locally made goods such as carved wood doors and furniture, wrought iron work (fences, room dividers, lighting fixtures, indoor and outdoor furniture), tile (floor, wall, and countertop), and leather goods. Colorful Mexican piñatas cost far less than those exported across the border, and they can be custom-made to your design. A great deal of pottery is made in Tijuana, as well as bongo drums, candles, hand-carved picture frames, bamboo furniture, sisal rugs, leather purses and wallets, onyx tabletops, artificial flowers, paintings on black velvet, and Italianate glassware.

You can watch glass blowers at work, using techniques unchanged since the sixteenth century, at the Inco Glass Factory on Revolución opposite the Frontón Palacio. Seats are provided for visitors in the kiln rooms behind the showroom. Hours are 10 a.m. to 10 p.m.

Savings can be made on many services. Beauty parlors and barber shops generally charge about half stateside prices. You can have eyeglasses made to your prescription, or your car reupholstered. Automobile body work is inexpensive if new parts are not involved. Facilities are minimal, and often your car's dents are hammered out right on the street.

The largest concentration of curio stores and gift-filled *pasajes* (arcades) is on Revolución Avenue between Second and Ninth and on its adjacent side streets. Local factories and fabricators scattered throughout the city are harder to find. Stop in at the sidewalk tourist booth on Revolución between Third and Fourth streets for information or check the yellow pages of the Tijuana telephone directory.

Friendly bargaining is expected at the smaller shops, while better quality stores generally have less flexible prices.

There are several large *panaderías* where you can stop for a snack or stock up on freshly baked rolls, cakes, cookies, and pastries to take back over the border.

Sports events. Horse races (admission $1) begin at noon on Saturdays and Sundays throughout the year at the racetrack on Agua Caliente Boulevard (Route 2 to Tecate). Greyhound races (admission 50¢) are at 7:45 p.m. Wednesdays through Saturdays and 7:15 p.m. on Sundays all year long. There is parimutuel betting.

Charreadas are held every Sunday at Cortijo San José (see page 16) and most Sundays during the summer at three other rings in town.

Jai alai *(hi-li)*, a Basque ball game, is played in the baroque Frontón Palacio on Revolución at Eighth Street. A fast-moving game something like handball, jai alai is played on a three-walled court. Each player wears a *cesta*—a long curved basket —strapped to one wrist; he catches the hard rubber ball in the *cesta* and returns it in a continuing motion. The ball reaches speeds of 150 miles per hour. Games are short, lasting about 15 minutes, and take place Thursday through Sunday evenings most of the year. There is parimutuel betting. Admission is 50 cents.

Bullfights are held every Sunday afternoon from the last Sunday in May until October, alternating between Tijuana's two rings: El Toreo, the older, downtown ring, and Plaza Monumental, on the Pacific, the second largest ring in the world. (The largest is in Mexico City.) Bloodless bullfights are held at Cortijo San José.

Where to stay. There are many hotels and motels in Tijuana, but most fall below American standards. Those who prefer to stay across the border in California will find several good motels in San Ysidro, within walking distance of the international border. Chula Vista and, of course, San Diego have many overnight accommodations.

Transportation. Aeronaves de Mexico makes daily flights to and from Los Angeles and La Paz via

AT INCO FACTORY master glass blower starts with "bubble" from kiln (right) to fashion a vase.

Tijuana. Aeronaves del Norte has daily flights between Tijuana and Mexicali.

Tijuana's taxis charge flat rates to specific destinations. Determine the rate before hiring a cab. If there's anything you can't find in town, Tijuana's cabbies are likely to know where it is.

Private bus lines operate within Tijuana. Buses also run from Tijuana to Tecate and Mexicali and down the Pacific Coast to Ensenada and on south as far as El Rosario.

The border highway

Border Highway 2 between Tijuana and Mexicali soars over Rodriguez dam 7 miles outside of Tijuana, then begins the long ascent of the western slope of the Sierra Juárez. You climb over low, chaparral-covered hills strewn with granite boul-

 THE RITUAL OF THE BULLFIGHT

The spectacle called the *fiesta brava*—the bullfight—is a highly ritualized drama dating back several centuries. Promptly at 4 p.m. the *paseo* (procession) signals the beginning of the event. Matadors, each dressed in his "suit of lights" (*traje de luces*) and followed by his paid banderilleros and picadors, parade into the ring and present themselves to the judge.

Each fight has three acts (or *tercios)* and lasts about 20 minutes. Trumpet blasts announce the beginning of an act. There are usually six fights in an afternoon; three matadors each kill two bulls.

The running of the bull begins a fight. *Peones* with capes run the bull around the ring so the matador can see how much spirit he has. (*El toro* must be four years old and weigh at least 900 pounds.) Then, using his silk cape, the matador leads the bull by a series of passes to one of the two mounted picadors. The picador thrusts a pic (lance) into the bull's tossing neck muscle to weaken it. Banderilleros stick pairs of short, decorated spears (banderillas) into the bull's withers to weaken him further.

The matador then proceeds to the part of the ritual called the *faena*. With his scarlet *muleta* (cape) the matador, working close to the horns, makes classic passes (*naturales, veronicas, chicuelinas* are some) to dominate the bull and wear him down. Then he aligns himself for the kill. Standing in front of the horns, he attempts to plunge his sword down between the shoulder blades and puncture the heart. A perfect *estocada* will kill the bull instantly.

ders and dip into small valleys dotted with live oaks. This is a wine-grape and olive-growing region with orderly vineyards and acres of olive groves.

Three miles west of Tecate you pass Rancho La Puerta, an attractive vacation-health resort where guests undergo a regimen of exercise as rugged as they choose, drink ranch-made grape cider, eat ranch-baked whole-wheat bread, and dine on vegetables in artful guises. The activities include jogging around the ranch's acres of grapes, hiking in the mountains, swimming, riding horseback, flying kites, and getting all wrapped up in hot herbal packs. Unlike other "beauty" resorts, which are feminine preserves, Rancho La Puerta is a family affair; there are almost as many men and children as women among the guests. Visitors are welcome. You can look around the ranch and have a vegetarian lunch in the dining room.

Tecate is a neat and pleasant town known for its pure spring water—and the Tecate and Carta Blanca beers brewed here. An untypical border town, devoid of commercialism, Tecate preserves, rather, small-town traditions. In summer its big event is a fair featuring folk dances, a parade, *charreadas*, carnival rides for children, and a bazaar selling Mexican handicrafts. Every summer weekend, after dark, the town park is the center for a festival of its own. Food is sold from stands, and there is music for dancing and entertainment.

If you want to avoid the long lines and congested traffic at the Tijuana border, you can cross the international boundary at Tecate with ease. The border is open from 8 a.m. to midnight. Across the border in California, State Route 94 goes northwest to San Diego and northeast to Interstate Route 8 and on to El Centro.

East of Tecate the road climbs gradually into piñon pine and granite country. Around La Rumorosa the road has been cut through a fantastic jumble of boulders. About a mile beyond the village you cross the peninsular divide and begin the steep, winding 4,000-foot descent of the Cantú grade. This is the most dramatic part of the road to Mexicali and one of the most spectacular mountain drives found anywhere. The vast desert of Laguna Salada can be seen some 25 miles away, and the Cocopah Mountains—partly covered by sand blown up from the desert floor—are visible beyond. In March the roadside is covered with purple lupine and yellow-flowered brittlebush, flowering sage, and handsome stands of ocotillo. In winter and spring, snow may fall in this area. The road becomes treacherous at such times.

At the bottom of the descent, the road winds over and around low-lying hills, then levels off when it reaches the desert floor and heads straight for Mexicali. To the left 1 mile you can see Pinto Mountain, where there is a petrified forest. On the out-

AT MUD VOLCANOES southeast of Mexicali you walk amid bubbling mud pots and pools in a lunar landscape.

skirts of Mexicali the highway passes by a row of shanties whose yards are a colorful jumble of drying clothes, old automobile parts, pigs and chickens, and children at play. The houses are humble, pieced together with scraps of wood and cardboard, but almost every one is surrounded by a blaze of flowers—sweet peas, sunflowers, and nasturtiums of incredible brightness and luxuriance.

Mexicali

As befits the capital of the state of Baja California, Mexicali is a city with great dignity and pride. There is little of the border-town brassiness of Tijuana, and there are few tourists. The city is the center of a vast agricultural empire that extends to the east and south. The water of the Colorado, diverted into irrigation channels, has transformed the sun-baked wastes of the Mexicali Valley into rich farmland. Cotton is king (the world's largest cotton gin is in Mexicali), but many other field crops and vegetables are grown in this land of perpetual sunshine.

For sportsmen and sun seekers, Mexicali is the gateway to San Felipe and the Sea of Cortez. Those who stop long enough to look around the city find broad boulevards and modern stores, office buildings, and fine residential homes. A small corner of the city is a cluster of enticements for tourists and night people. Almost as soon as you cross the inter-national boundary from Calexico you reach Melgar Street, the center of curio stores, neon night clubs, and tawdry bars. The stores sell everything from horrors to good handicrafts. The nightspots offer a similar range of entertainment.

East along Obregón Avenue and adjacent east-west avenues is the modern Mexicali of concrete-and-glass stores and cinema palaces. In the center is the impressive stone Palacio de Gobierno, where the affairs of the state of Baja California are conducted. Mexicali's brewery is a couple of blocks south. Despite all the new construction, Mexicali still retains the street scenes that give older Mexican cities their flavor. Open-air stands overflow with fruits, vegetables, and chiles. Vendors carry stacks of bamboo cages filled with finches and canaries. In the large city market on Obregón and Calle A, a profusion of wares is sold in separate stalls.

During winter *charros* display their horsemanship at a ring east of Calzada Justo Sierra on Compuertes. The *charreadas* (rodeos) are irregularly held on holidays and Sundays and often are not scheduled far in advance.

Club Deportivo Campestra, a couple of miles out of town west of Route 5 (San Felipe highway), has a modern 18-hole golf course. Also on the grounds is Laguna Mexico, a popular lake for boating and water skiing. The golf course is closed in summer. While Mexicali is pleasantly warm in winter and spring, in summer it sizzles—temperatures may soar to 120. Everyone who can gets out of town.

Mud volcanoes

An easy side trip from Mexicali is Volcano Lake (Laguna de los Volcanes), 25 miles southeast of the city. This is an area approximately 2 by 5 miles with hot bubbling pools and miniature volcanoes several feet high spewing out mud and steam. You walk amid the pools on a crust of mud and salt. Step too near the pools and the hard surface cracks like ice or sinks like mud beneath your feet. Some of the pools are white, yellow, or orange. Others are black and viscous. In the most violently bubbling pools, volcanic gases force the mud up in jets. Some of the mud spatter cones are inert; steam guides you to the active ones.

There is a strong, acrid smell of sulphur. The continuous roaring and hissing of the dozens of government steam wells that are converting this source of energy into electricity sound like a weird choir from another world. Volcano Lake has been described as a scene straight out of Dante's *Inferno*.

The mud pots and hot springs are believed to be the result of water seeping to hot volcanic rocks not far below the surface. Next to Yellowstone Park, this may be the largest hydrothermal area of its kind on the North American continent.

To reach the mud volcanoes, go east from Mexicali on Route 2 for 6 miles beyond the junction of routes 2 and 5, turn south on the paved road, and continue for 14 miles through the village of Hidalgo to the federal gas company (Campo Geotermico). A short distance beyond the entrance, leave the paved road where it crosses the railroad tracks and follow the dirt road that parallels the tracks. In just over 3 miles you will come to the turnoff to the village of Pasquale (also called Patzcuaro); turn right and drive through the village and on about 2 miles, or as far as you can go. From here on you have to hike. Wear old shoes, because you'll sink up to your ankles in mud.

THE PACIFIC COAST

Two good paved roads along the scenic shore connect Tijuana and Ensenada. Old Highway 1 takes an inland route as far as Rosarito, skirts the coast for 21 miles, then swings inland again. The limited-access toll Highway 1D follows the coast all the way. There are three tollgates: Tijuana's El Monumental gate, 60 cents for cars and pickup trucks (76 cents with trailer); the Rosarito gate, 80 cents ($1 with trailer); and the San Miguel gate, $1 ($1.24 with trailer). Mileages are the same but the toll road is faster, particularly on weekends and holidays when traffic on the old road may be heavy.

South of Ensenada the highway winds through hilly countryside cultivated with olives, grapes, and grain. Pavement ends in 90 miles. Below this point the dusty main highway can be slow going, even for high-clearance vehicles. The surface was built up for paving several years ago but has deteriorated into axle-deep chuckholes. Since there are few culverts and no bridges, rains wash big arroyos in the roadbed. But along the coast where few travelers venture lie magnificent beaches.

Tijuana to Ensenada

Those who remember the shoreline from Tijuana to Ensenada as lonely and unspoiled, with only a few beach resorts and communities, would have difficulty recognizing it today. The sandy beaches are still there, but the once-empty bluffs have sprouted developments. As far south as La Misión, the coast is a nearly continuous hodgepodge of motels, trailer parks, mobile home communities, campgrounds, cafes, subdivisions, and fishing shanties. Southern Californians, pressed for surfing and fishing space on overcrowded beaches at home, stream to the northern coast on holidays and weekends. Many have leased or rented ocean-view lots, setting up camp in everything from junk trailers to high-priced homes.

A few beach resorts are modern and well equipped, but more offer less appealing accommodations and often are overpriced. Some so-called "trailer parks" have no hook-ups or water. Almost every undeveloped cove or bluff has become an "instant" campground merely by the presence of someone who collects a dollar or two. The facilities are minimal or nonexistent.

While the upper coast is rapidly developing, less accessible stretches of shore between La Misión and San Miguel remain wild. This area is one of the most spectacular shoreline drives on the peninsula. The highway clings to sheer cliffs high above the Pacific, and the views of sea and surf and craggy cliffs on a sunny day are breathtaking.

One of the principal resorts between Tijuana and Ensenada is Rosarito, a popular beach community. The Rosarito Beach Hotel, built in the 1920's, has hotel rooms and bungalows, a 100-foot swimming pool (also a children's pool), a tennis court, and horses for riding on the beach. A short, partly paved airstrip parallels the beach in front of the hotel. Pottery shops line the old highway north and south of town. Speed limits are strictly enforced in Rosarito.

Farther south are Popotla, a trailer park community with mobile home rentals and a pool; Cantamar, a motel and trailer park with a restaurant, pool, and entertainment; Half Way House, a cafe at an old stage stop; and La Fonda, a motel with a restaurant, on a hill overlooking the beach.

At La Misión are the ruins of mission San Miguel. Playa La Misión is a private development of retirement homes on leased lots.

San Miguel Village is a large development of beachfront homes, trailer park, restaurant, private and public campgrounds. There are boat rentals, a launching ramp, and riding on miles of trails. An invitational surfing meet is held here annually.

Tecate to Ensenada

Travelers westbound from Mexicali to Ensenada can take a scenic shortcut on paved Highway 3 south from Tecate. This pleasant drive takes you through rolling hills, pastures rimmed with oaks, and occasional vineyards and olive groves.

At the community of El Testerazo, about 31 miles south of Tecate, several yards display wood carvings within sight of the highway. El Testerazo has become a center for distinctive primitive sculptures —animal forms; heads that look half human, half demonic, and often are humorous; and carvings that resemble small totem poles. The sculptures are sold in curio stores in the border towns and are exported to the United States. A "Baja Man" 20 inches high that sells for $40 north of the border can be bought in El Testerazo for $12. With a rough finish, sculptures of this size sell for as little as $6. The master carver is Leopoldo Arcoz, who learned his craft in Mexico City. About 10 years ago he began to teach woodcarving to others in El Testerazo.

Seventeen miles beyond El Testerazo is Guadalupe, once a sizable Russian settlement. In 1906 a group of Molokans sought refuge here after breaking with the Russian Orthodox Church and the Czar. The small colony retained many native customs and costumes. In recent years the Mexican Government has moved large numbers of Mexican nationals into the area in its agrarian reform program, and most of the Russians have left, the majority migrating to Los Angeles. Only a Russian cemetery and a park remain as reminders of the past.

Ensenada

The best way to see Ensenada for the first time is to park your car and take a leisurely stroll down Calle Primera, the main tourist thoroughfare. Parallel to it and creating a delightful setting for shopping excursions are Ensenada's picturesque harbor and beach. Ocean breezes and early morning fog keep the town cool all summer; winters are usually mild. Allow enough time to see the harbor, with its sportfishing boats and private yachts, and to have a stand-up seafood lunch on the wharf at fish row.

MASTER CARVER of El Testerazo sands a wood figure. Sculptures are displayed along highway.

A horseback ride down the beach also makes a pleasant diversion from shopping. Horses rent for $1 an hour and can be found where Arroyo de Ensenada crosses Calle Primera.

In the shops that line Primera and Avenida Ruíz, you will find a good variety of Mexican craftwork as well as foreign imports. Prices vary considerably, from about half of what you might expect to pay north of the border to no savings at all. The better Mexican crafts include Tonalá and Oaxacan pottery, Guadalajara glass, and Taxco silver. Many shops stock piñatas, popular with Christmas shoppers, and there's an open-air stand specializing in all kinds of basketwork.

On the other side of Primera from the Bahía Hotel (and in back of the block) is Ensenada's *charro* ring. If you happen to be in town on a weekend or holiday, stop at the ring to see if a *charreada* has been scheduled. There is usually someone around tending the horses. The Mexican version of the rodeo is a thrilling spectator sport—and one largely overlooked by Americans. While the time

CHARROS, *or "gentlemen cowboys," wearing the broad-brimmed hats that are their trademark, show off roping skill in Ensenada ring. Rodeo-like* charreadas *are popular in border towns.*

and day vary, *charreadas* are held almost every holiday afternoon and on occasional Saturdays or Sundays in summer. Sometimes it is not known until the day of the event whether a performance will occur. If the *charreada* is for a special benefit, the admission is usually about $1.

Two of the most colorful of Ensenada's many fiestas are La Posada, from December 16 to Christmas Eve, and Mardi Gras, held on the four days preceding Ash Wednesday. They are celebrated by parades, costumes, and music.

Situated at the north end of 10-mile-wide Todos Santos Bay, Ensenada is ideally located for water-oriented activities. The town is known as the "yellowtail capital of the world" and has a large fleet of sport-fishing boats which in summer go after not only yellowtail but barracuda, sea bass, bonito, corvina, and other game fish. The Annual Newport-Ensenada International Yacht Race is timed to end in Ensenada on May 5, the day Mexico defeated the French in 1863. When the 400 to 500 entrants fill the bay, it is a sight to see. Surf fishing and swimming are popular along the 10 miles of beach which line the bay and Punta Estero below the town, and many trailer parks are being developed along these beaches. Surfing north and south of Ensenada has increased in popularity, and meets

are now held in the area every year.

There is good hunting in the area for quail, duck, and geese.

Mexico's largest winery, Bodegas de Santo Tomás, occupies several blocks in the heart of downtown Ensenada on Avenida Machero, two blocks from Avenida Juárez. Founded in 1888, it takes its name from the valley to the south where most of its grapes are grown. (Some wine grapes also come from the Guadalupe area.) The winery produces 24 varieties of wines, brandies, and vermouths. Except during the month of July, when it closes, the winery is open to visitors. Tours are conducted. Perhaps the best time for a visit is September, when the grapes are being pressed. Californians can't take Santo Tomás wines across the border, but several liquor stores and supermarkets in the San Diego area carry the label.

The restaurants in Ensenada use water from deep wells in the hills in back of town. It is bottled locally. You can buy water directly from the bottling plant.

Where to stay. Ensenada is the closest thing in Baja to an American-style vacation resort. Only La Paz offers a comparable choice of modern hotels, motels, and restaurants. But Ensenada, because it is

PINATAS in whimsical animal forms attract shopper in Ensenada. You fill them with candy, toys.

so easily reached by highway from the border, has many more—at last count, over 50. Several of the better ones are on Calle Primera next to the beach. There is also a resort at Estero Beach south of town. (Rates for all are on file in the Department of Tourism on Calle Primera in Ensenada; go to the office to obtain them.)

In addition to the trailer parks north and south of town on the bay and at Punta Banda, open camping is permitted on the beach from Playa Hermosa to the military camp and on Punta Estero. Near Maneadero there is a good private campground, and there is open camping on the way to San Carlos Hot Springs.

Road to San Carlos Hot Springs

Agua Caliente San Carlos—one of two hot springs resorts in the Ensenada area—is reached by a dirt road that winds through a narrow and densely vegetated canyon. A year-round stream flows through the canyon and across the road. The summer gardens of small farms en route are luxuriant with tomatoes, peppers, and corn.

After 7 miles and a stream crossing, there is a well-kept campground beside a dammed section of the stream, each site with a table and benches under a grape arbor ($1, if you use the firewood stacked at each fireplace). The toilet facilities are primitive. In the next 5 miles there are a few places where you can pick out a campsite in a streamside thicket or under massive live oaks.

The developed hot springs at road's end has mineral baths, a swimming pool, a line of not-too-private cabins, and space for tent and trailer campers. (Rates start at $2; the pool and baths carry an additional charge.) In summer, when every available space is taken, you may have the feeling you are camped in a public bath.

Punta Banda

West of the large agricultural community of Maneadero the ruggedly beautiful peninsula of Punta Banda juts into the Pacific, forming the southern boundary of Todos Santos Bay. Sandy at sea level on the sheltered inner shore, Punta Banda ascends to mountain ridges surpassing 1,200 feet, where rocky terraces and sheer cliffs drop to the churning waters below. The paved road to the sea spout called La Bufadora passes several developed camp-and-trailer parks on the beach where you can rent a small boat or launch your own for fishing and skin-diving in the bay. One campground is on a marine terrace reached by a steeply pitched road. Rock fishing is superb. Farther out on Punta Banda, open camping is permitted on unposted land. Some of the most striking coastal scenery can be seen only by hiking or riding over the brushy slopes. (Horses sometimes can be rented for $1 an hour at several places along the highway.) High on the windy hills are magnificent views of the Pacific, Ensenada with its mountain backdrop, and the wild, jagged coastline south.

The road terminates at a rocky cove with steep cliffs, offshore skerries with gulls and sea lions, and the surge of spray from La Bufadora—"the buffalo snort." This large sea spout (a short distance beyond a parking lot) is formed by heavy ocean swells funneled into a narrow gorge that ends in a tunnel. The resulting pressure forces the water up through an opening with a terrific roar and a whoosh. La Bufadora puts on its best show during a south wind in December and when there are heavy sea swells. It may spout a hundred feet or more, covering cliffs and spectators alike with a cold spray.

La Bufadora is a popular attraction for families on outings, and in summer and on weekends vendors nearby conduct a brisk business in giant conch shells, dried pufferfish, and the weird skeletons of stingrays. If you see a stand surrounded by children, it will probably belong to a *churro* maker.

Using a machine that resembles a sausage stuffer, he grinds out long spirals of dough into boiling fat. The puffy brown strips are then rolled in sugar and cut in long pieces. *Churros* taste like crisp crullers, only they're better, and they're as habit-forming as peanuts.

Near La Bufadora are several restaurants serving freshly caught lobster and abalone, in season, and fish; a well-developed trailer park; a boat concessionaire; and a dive shop that rents skin-diving equipment. While some people still dive for lobster and abalone in the reefs offshore, it is now illegal.

Maneadero to San Quintín

Just below Maneadero is a check station. A tourist card is required to travel farther south. It is wise to complete the formalities at the border, but you can obtain a card (with proof of citizenship or a birth certificate) at the station here. The immigration officer may simply ask for a dollar and have you record your license plate number; however, it is illegal for you to travel beyond this point without a tourist card.

About 19 miles south of Maneadero is the picturesque village of Santo Tomás, known all over Mexico for the wines that bear its name. Acres of Zinfandels, Chenin Blancs, Barberas, and other grapes surround the village. The Dominicans, who established a mission in Santo Tomás in 1791, were the valley's first vintners. Barely a trace remains of the old mission, but the growing of grapes for wine continues. The early-autumn harvest is transported by truck a short distance to the large Ensenada winery.

The drive from Santo Tomás to Colnett winds through rolling chaparral-covered slopes and coastal mountains with a pastoral beauty much like that of southern California before it was bulldozed, developed, and freewayed. You pass well-tended grapevines bordered by silvery groves of olives and farmyards filled with goats, chickens, and children.

Puerto Santo Tomás, about 19 miles from the paved main highway, is the first of several accessible areas along the coast between Punta Banda and San Quintín. The sea-carved cliffs and crashing combers here are typical of the rugged character of this coast. To reach Puerto Santo Tomás you leave Highway 1 about 2 miles north of the town of Santo Tomás.

SPRAYING AND ROARING "La Bufadora," a large sea spout, elicits squeals as it gives children a shower.

At other places along this shore you will find sandy coves and long, dune-backed beaches; rocky areas usually have tidal pools, sometimes sea caves, sculptured arches, and sea spouts. About 17 miles past Santo Tomás, a dirt road heads southwest to the twin oceanside villages of San Isidro and Erendira. Punta Cabras, 6 miles north, has good Pismo clamming and surf fishing, and boats are available for rent.

At the village of Colnett, a right turn at the church a quarter mile past Bradley's gas station and restaurant takes you to San Antonio del Mar, an extensive sweep of dunes and sandy beach popular for clamming and fishing.

Farther south is the rapidly growing community of Colonia Guerrero, the agricultural center for the entire valley. The main road from here to El Rosario is filled with chuckholes, dips, and ruts. It is silty and dusty when dry, impassable when wet. In some places you have to proceed at a crawl to avoid breaking an axle. You wave to children walking along the road as you lurch by, only to see them again moments later as they pass you. Most traffic takes to the roadside ditches, which have fewer ruts. The worst holes are in a 12-mile stretch from San Quintín south. A somewhat better road can be followed inland at Colonia Cárdenas, through San Simón, and back to the main highway, avoiding the most nerve-wracking stretch.

San Quintín

Beautiful San Quintín (pronounced keen-TEEN) is a nearly landlocked bay well known to duck hunters. In winter it is the home of thousands of ducks and black brant. There are excellent clamming and surf fishing on the ocean side. Diving for lobster and abalone is done in the rocks at the mouth of the bay. There is ocean sport-fishing for giant black sea bass, white sea bass, yellowtail, and other game fish near San Martín Island. The best weather is in July and August. The bay waters, sheltered and rather shallow, provide protected anchorage for small boats.

The biggest season of the year at San Quintín is November through February, when hunters come for black brant shooting. The bay, which has one of the largest concentrations of brant on the Pacific Coast, is a favorite wintering spot for these Arctic-breeding geese. White-winged doves are also hunted in the winter months.

Although the land around San Quintín is divided into *ejidos*, the bay area itself is undeveloped. Many roads, crisscrossing in every direction, lead to the inner bay, and most are far smoother than the rutted main highway. To reach the upper bay where two motels—Ernesto's and The Old Mill—sit side by side at water's edge, turn off the main highway at the trailer park (with red-brick arches). Across the highway are two large tanks. Follow the dirt road for 4 miles.

Above the motels, roads lead to the opposite shore of the bay and beyond to the salt works and the ocean. Dune buggies and four-wheel-drive vehicles can follow the peninsula south by driving along the beach at low tide. If you plan to go exploring in this area, fill up with gas and allow plenty of time. There are so many roads, all unmarked, you're bound to become lost.

A sandy road south of the motels follows the shore of the bay past flats teeming with shore birds, high bluffs, boggy meadows, and marshes of eel grass—the favorite food of the wintering black brant.

Ernesto's and The Old Mill are the principal places to stay on the bay. You can launch your own boat at the motel ramps. A landing strip here is shared by both motels.

Ernesto's offers both American and European plans. Rates vary, depending on the season; the highest rate is $12 a day per person, American plan, or $8 a day for two, European plan. Rooms with kitchens are $12.50 a day for two. A charter fishing boat (for four) to San Martín Island costs $50 a day.

The Old Mill Motel, also with both American and European plan, is $11 a day per person, American plan, $6 a day for two, European plan. Rooms with kitchens are $8 a day for two. A 40-foot party boat and a Navy PT boat can be rented at rates varying from $25 for two to $40 for five. There is space for trailers and truck campers, with electricity and water hookups. The Old Mill Motel occupies the original site of a mill built by a group of English colonizers. Most of the old frame buildings are gone, but on the grounds is the steam engine that provided power for the mill.

San Quintín to El Rosario

Below San Quintín stretches a long, wide beach of drifting gray dunes. Pismo clams can easily be dug on a minus tide. A low, sandy bluff provides some shelter for camping. You can reach the beach area through Santa María Sky Ranch (a motel now closed) or by roads south of the ranch. Several motels are under construction in this area.

About 10 miles below El Socorro, a lease-colony of American homes, is the rocky wash of Arroyo Hondo, a favorite of campers. The windy bluffs above the arroyo provide spectacular views of pounding surf and long white combers below. There is continuous beach camping from Arroyo Hondo to El Consuelo in the lee of sculptured cliffs.

El Rosario

On the edge of a broad river valley leading to the sea is the small farming town of El Rosario, the last oceanside settlement on the main transpeninsular highway—and the beginning of the great central desert. El Rosario is really two communities—Rosario de Arriba, the principal settlement on the north bank of the arroyo, and Rosario de Abajo, a mile and a half downstream. Many travelers stop at "Espinosa's Place" for information and advice about the area and road conditions ahead. Meals and simple lodgings are available. In the living room is an impressive ammonite, a fossil cephalopod dug from an extensive marine deposit in the Santa Catarina Landing area.

You cross the stream to reach Rosario de Abajo. Adjoining the plaza of Rosario de Abajo are old ruins and a new chapel. A road past the chapel follows the coastal hills for about 10 miles to Punta Baja, a fishing camp on a bluff overlooking a beautiful sandy strand.

In recent years, El Rosario has been the site of important paleontological discoveries. Tons of bones of mammoth 50-foot-long hadrosaurian or "duckbill" dinosaurs that roamed lagoons and playas here about 73 million years ago have been dug out of the "badlands," an extensive area of deeply eroded mesas bordering the beach. If you hike through the canyons in back of the beach, you may find small pieces of dinosaur bone which have eroded out of the cliffs.

Two places in El Rosario sell gas. Compare prices, because they may vary considerably. This is the last real pump for more than 300 miles.

THE GULF COAST

A fast 127-mile paved road to the sport-fishing village of San Felipe brings the Sea of Cortez within a three or four-hour drive of the California border. One of the best food and game fishes anywhere, the totuava, is caught in the northern end of the Cortez. Below San Felipe a sandy road passes many secluded beaches and primitive fishing camps en route to Puertecitos, a small colony of American-leased homes and trailers. Passenger cars cannot safely be driven beyond this point on the Gulf coast.

The paved road to San Felipe is an interesting drive in March and April when the severe desert springs to life with green leaves and wildflowers. The air is fresh and clear, and the days are warm. For the first 20 miles you skirt the edge of the fertile farmland of the Colorado delta. To the east is the dark volcanic cone of Cerro Prieto, the landmark for an extensive area of sulphuric springs and bubbling mud pots. On the west are the bleak and barren Cocopahs, a mountain range bordering the eastern expanse of Laguna Salada.

Soon the highway comes within sight of Río Hardy, a winding backwater of the Colorado. Several river resorts are situated on its brushy banks, the principal ones being Campo Río Hardy and El Mayor. At Campo Río Hardy, there is a small store and bar selling soft drinks, beer, and snacks; an outdoor terrace overlooks the river. Camping ramadas range from $1 to $4 a night, depending on their proximity to the river, and cabins from $4 to $11. Lots here are leased on an annual basis as trailer or cabin sites for about $120.

Fishermen will find catfish and bass in the river. In season there is hunting for dove, quail, ducks, and geese. Rowboats (without motors) can be rented for $4 a day.

South of Río Hardy, the highway traverses a desolate stretch of sand dunes and crusty salt flats spreading to the Gulf, with richly colored volcanic mountains on the west. Mexicans call this arid area El Desierto de Los Chinos, for the group of Chinese immigrants who began a trek from San Felipe to Mexicali in 1902 to find work. Incredibly, they attempted the journey in August, when temperatures made the desert an inferno. All but eight of the 42 perished of thirst and heat exhaustion.

Forbidding for much of the year, this desert in early spring puts on a brief but bright display of color. Ocotillo covers the plains like hundreds of Christmas candles, and clumps of brittlebush massed with daisylike flowers are a golden haze disappearing in the horizon. Along the roadside grow sand verbena, lupine, prickly poppies, and apricot mallow. Exquisite white desert lilies brighten the sandy bluffs along the Gulf.

North of San Felipe, where the highway passes close to the Gulf, there are a couple of beachside trailer parks—and many open camping spots—that offer a little more privacy than some sites closer to the town. A new resort community is under construction 4 miles north of San Felipe.

San Felipe

The first natural bay on the Baja side of the Sea of Cortez, San Felipe is the principal boat access to waters of the upper Gulf. Many game fish, including the giant totuava (which spawns in the mouth of the Colorado River), are caught here—some year round. Surf fishing is also good and produces an occasional totuava. Summers are oppressively hot, but from October through May the weather is warm and it seldom rains.

The paved road from the border to San Felipe village makes it possible for many people to trailer their own boats. For those who don't there are ren-

BELOW SAN FELIPE buggies and bikes are often seen running on the beach and climbing dunes.

WHIPLIKE OCOTILLOS are characteristic of northern Gulf coast. For short time in spring, green-leafed ocotillo and colorful wildflowers brighten this sandy desert.

THE TIDE really goes out at San Felipe. Shrimp trawler and other beached boats will be afloat with the next high tide.

ROCK OYSTERS can be gathered at low tide below Puertecitos; all you need are hammer and chisel.

tal skiffs and motors and also charter boats ($50 to $70 a day). This part of the Cortez has 23 to 28-foot rise and fall of tides, creating a demand for a unique business. The outgoing tide leaves fishermen's boats high and dry on the beach. When their owners are ready to use them again, Mexicans with old jalopies tow them to water's edge and refloat them for a fee.

Heavily damaged by a hurricane that roared up from the lower Gulf in 1967, San Felipe quickly rebuilt itself into a bigger town. However, it is still basically a fishing camp, not a luxury resort, and you'll find the prices lower than elsewhere in Baja. Fishermen (many with their families) come in trailers or campers, and some simply camp on the beach—particularly on holidays. Rates at the four motels begin at about $5 single, $6 double. Reflecting demand, there are at least twice as many trailer parks as motels.

Most people come to fish, but the miles of beaches and dunes also are attracting an increasing number who come to ride dune buggies and motorbikes. A store in town rents bikes. There is also horseback riding on the beach.

San Felipe's bay is busy with shrimp boats in winter and spring. A couple of *pescaderías* in town sell unshelled shrimp by the kilo for less than $2, as well as other freshly caught fish and shellfish.

In the inland desert and along the cliffs and beaches that line the Gulf, camping is excellent—even in midwinter. April and May can be windy. San Felipe also makes a good headquarters and supply point for trips to canyons on the eastern slopes of the San Pedro Mártir and lower Juárez mountains.

Drinking water is bottled at a plant in town. The liquor stores sometimes carry spring water in plastic jugs brought in from the States.

Puertecitos

Pavement gives way to dirt and sand south of San Felipe, but passenger cars and trailers usually have little trouble traveling to Puertecitos. For the first 15 miles the road is flat and sandy; then it becomes bumpier and gravelly, and occasionally rocky. The coastal desert vegetation is rich and varied—ocotillo, large palo verdes and smoke trees, wildflowers in spring, and clumps of columnar cacti with bearded tips the Mexicans call *senita,* or "old man." There are beautiful swimming and camping beaches en route (the white sands of Percebu are particularly appealing) and a half dozen primitive fishing resorts with private campgrounds. Beachcombing can be rewarding: The sands are littered with shells and large keyhole sand dollars. Highly polished one to two-inch olive shells are found on some of these beaches.

At a natural cove 52 miles south of San Felipe, the road becomes treacherous as it begins an ascent over hills of lava rock. House trailers and trailered boats cannot safely be taken beyond this point, so some Americans have come this far and set up housekeeping on lots, for which they pay about $70 a year. Despite the property signs—like one that reads "El Cajon City Limits"—this village is Puertecitos.

Puertecitos has a *cantina,* gas pump, and landing strip. The fishing is good—if you take a quick stroll down the beach past the cottages, almost anyone you stop to talk with will have a fish story that happened that morning. Fishing in these waters is best in summer, but the weather then is hot. Temperatures are usually in the 80's and 90's but soar to 115 when the wind changes to westerly. The best weather comes in October and November and in the spring months.

Puertecitos has a 22-foot rise and fall of tide which catches some fishermen by surprise. They beach their boats in front of the *cantina* for lunch and come out later to find them stranded.

Hot sulphur springs around the point from the boat-launching ramp feed a huge tidepool and form a natural bath often used for bathing. The pool is flooded by seawater and also cleaned out at high tide, then warms up as the tide goes out.

THE INTERIOR

The little-known interior of northern Baja is a cool country of pine-forested plateaus, craggy peaks, and grassy mountain meadows. Two extensive mountain ranges form the backbone of the upper peninsula—the Sierra Juárez and the Sierra San Pedro Mártir, both a continuation of the San Jacinto mountains of Southern California. The western sides of the ranges slope gradually to the Pacific; on the east the drop is abrupt, with sheer escarpments thousands of feet high gashed with canyons, some filled with palms.

Most accessible is the Juárez in the north, a flat plateau about 5,500 feet high with few prominent peaks. A maze of dirt roads meanders across the plateau down into the foothills and valleys past scattered ranches, farming villages, and a few Indian settlements.

The higher, wilder San Pedro Mártir to the south is reached by a road below Colnett on the Pacific coast and the San Felipe-Ensenada road, which passes through the only gap between the two ranges. The high country of the San Pedro Mártir is a wilderness of peaks that challenge mountain climbers, with trails for backpackers and burros.

Sierra de Juárez

The most popular spot in the plateau country of the Sierra Juárez is Laguna Hanson, a natural mountain lake in a scenic setting of tall Jeffrey pines. Massive granite boulders, worn into strange shapes, are scattered in and around the lake and in the forest clearings, singly and in precarious balancing stacks. On the edge of the lake are campsites where you can put up a tent on a soft bed of pine needles that have a distinctive sweet vanilla scent. There are rustic picnic tables and fireplaces, and trash cans—rare objects in Baja—are even provided. Laguna Hanson is the only public picnic and camping area of its kind on the peninsula.

The shallow lake, about a half mile wide, is sometimes a shining expanse of water, other times little more than a wet meadow. The amount of water depends on winter snows and summer rains. In winter the lake freezes over. Snow falls in the area

LAGUNA HANSON, surrounded by pines and giant boulders in the heart of Sierra Juarez, may be marshy in summer, frozen in winter. This is a popular picnicking and camping area.

from December through April and may reach a depth of two feet.

Laguna Hanson, also called Laguna de Juárez, has been designated as part of Parque Nacional Constitución de 1857. The lake can be reached from either the north or south by dirt roads; late-model passenger cars travel them regularly.

From the south, the lake is 55 miles from Ensenada. You turn off the Ensenada-San Felipe road past Ojos Negros and follow the signs to Aserradero. The road passes through a lovely live oak canyon, gradually climbs through piñon pine and juniper country, and reaches the high pine plateau. At Aserradero, an active lumber camp 3 miles south of Laguna Hanson, logging roads go in every direction. After you pass a huge pile of sawdust and cross a dip, turn left, then take the first right (you will pass a gas pump).

From the north, two dirt roads turn off Highway 2 to Laguna Hanson—one at El Cóndor, the other near La Rumorosa. They join 23 miles from Laguna Hanson. The El Cóndor road is easily found at Route 2, but the lower part is poorer than the Rumorosa road. The turn from near La Rumorosa, however, is difficult to find and at last report was unmarked. It is 1.4 miles west of the Servicio Alaska gas station on the main highway and .3 miles west of a building with a sign "Industria Caliza Bastidas." Once found, the road is well posted to Aserradero. The distance to Laguna Hanson is 40 miles.

Canyons of the eastern slope

Between the Juárez and Cocopah ranges the dry lake bed known as Laguna Salada extends 30 to 40 miles in length and up to 15 in width. Like the Salton sink in California, it is below sea level and was once an arm of the Gulf of California. The surface of the lake, when dry, makes easy, fast driving. A maze of roads crosses the lake bed and provides access to the palm canyons in the eastern escarpment of the Sierra Juárez. The roads are unmarked, and it is very difficult to find and stay on the one you want. The most heavily traveled or most recently scraped road is usually the best choice. After a rain, sections of Laguna Salada are impassable.

A few of the palm canyons, like Guadalupe and Cantú Palms, can be reached directly by road and are fairly easy to find. The others, like Tajo, La Mora, Palomar, and Santa Isabel, can be elusive. If you set out to explore any of them, plan on getting lost. There is no gas in the area, so keep a large reserve. It is wise to have plenty of water and extra provisions. Even veteran desert explorers run into trouble in Laguna Salada. There is deep sand on all sides of the lake bed. Except for Guadalupe Canyon

and Cantú Palms, four-wheel-drive vehicles are needed to reach most of the palm canyons.

In summer these canyons are like ovens, but from about October to May they are pleasantly warm and make interesting places to camp, explore, and hike. As recently as the first decade of this century, the Cocopah Indians migrated up and down the canyons with the seasons. The bedrock mortars they used for grinding palm seeds and mesquite beans are commonly seen. There are many petroglyphs and pictographs, and in the less frequently visited canyons there is a great deal of broken pottery still lying around Indian rock shelters.

Guadalupe Canyon. The only commercially developed canyon on the eastern slope of the Sierra Juárez is Guadalupe, 37 miles south of Route 2 via a dirt road (signs mark the way). Hot mineral waterfalls flow out of solid rock in the hillside here, and there are pools covered by palm-thatched cabanas where you can soak in hot sulphur water. A spring has been dammed to form a large swimming pool. There are many campsites, some along the palm-shaded stream—which is as inviting to rattlesnakes as to campers. On a holiday weekend Guadalupe usually is jammed. The camping fee, which includes use of the mineral baths and the pool, is $2 a day on weekdays, $3 a day on weekends.

The canyon itself, wild and undeveloped, is reached from the baths on a short trail. A stream of good, sweet-tasting water flows through the canyon between smooth white granite boulders and stately palms. Most of the palms are *Washingtonia filifera*, but some are the smaller blue fan palms, *Erythea armata*, a type not found north of the border. As you ascend the canyon, you discover small waterfalls, and the sides of the streambed and the slopes are green with tamarisks, palo verdes, and small elephant trees. In spring clumps of blue and yellow wildflowers grow in the sandy stretches beside the stream.

The canyon narrows, and its vertical walls of solid rock rise higher until they end at a high waterfall that plunges into a deep, clear pool. Circling around the waterfall to its top, the canyon resumes rising past several other falls until it reaches the top of the range. Here Laguna Hanson can be seen in the distance.

Cantú Palms. Petroglyphs, bedrock metates, and rock shelters littered with potsherds are the still-visible evidence of the Indians who once lived in the area of Cantú Palms. Turn right at Rancho La Poderosa (about 17 miles from Highway 2 on the same road you take to Guadalupe). The canyon is 1.3 miles from here and the palms can be seen from this road. Two areas have palms, and water can be seen seeping out of the ground in places. Named for a former governor, Cantú Palms has an abandoned quartz mine and sometimes is used as a camp by wood gatherers. From the palms one has a sweeping view of the dry lake and the Cocopah range.

Ensenada to San Felipe

San Matias Pass is the only gap in the mountainous backbone of Baja's upper peninsula, and an east-west road through the pass enables you to drive from Ensenada on the Pacific to San Felipe on the Gulf. The road is a series of well-worn dirt paths connecting ranches and farm communities, rambling all over the countryside before reaching San Felipe. Though it has the usual chuckholes, rough surfaces, and rocky spots, part of the way it is smooth and fast. However, in the less-traveled interior, sections of the road deteriorate and are so narrow that your vehicle is scratched by sharp, thorny roadside brush.

The most serious driving problem is staying on the main road. There are many unmarked intersections, and it is easy to take a wrong turn and not know it for miles. North of Valle Trinidad the road becomes rough as it makes a steep descent over sharp bedrock to the valley. Standard passenger cars should not attempt this road, although they can make it from Valle Trinidad to San Felipe and from Ensenada to Laguna Hanson via Ojos Negros.

The road will be paved eventually (the government says in five years). So far only the first 10 miles from Ensenada are paved, and this deteriorates so badly into chuckholes after 7 miles that the dirt road comes as a relief. It crosses the coastal range—through scenery similar to back-country southern California. After 15 miles you reach a side road to Agua Caliente hot springs. Rounding the top of the coastal range there are sweeping views of the Ojos Negros Valley below and the Sierra Juárez range in the distance. The road descends into the valley and picks up a wide dirt road to Ojos Negros. First you pass an old store, then several miles beyond some newer buildings—a small chapel and store.

Between Ojos Negros and Valle Trinidad you pass close to two of Baja's largest Indian settlements—La Huerta, the home of about 75 Tipais,

GUADALUPE is one of several palm canyons on east side of Sierra Juarez. Going gets steeper beyond here.

PAIPAIS of Santa Catarina are among few indigenous Indians left on the peninsula. Their wattle-and-daub houses often are built against giant boulders which serve as walls and resist earthquakes.

and Santa Catarina, a settlement of some 150 Paipais. Thousands of Indians lived on the peninsula when the Spanish first arrived in the sixteenth century, but only about 500 descendants remain. Most are Paipais, Tipais (Digueños), and Kiliwas living in small scattered settlements in the highlands north of Valle Trinidad. Their homes are thatched huts with walls made of adobe or willow branches, and their basic food consists of tortillas, *frijoles*, and what nuts, berries, fruits (cactus), and seeds they can collect. They hunt deer and rabbit. The women used to make clay ollas like those found in rock shelters in the eastern canyons of the Juárez, but now pottery-making is confined largely to clay whistles.

The Dominicans built their last mission in Baja at Santa Catarina in 1797 around a tribe of approximately 1,500 Paipais. In a series of revolts the Indians killed all the missionaries except those who fled. They burned the mission in 1840—today only mounds remain to outline where the walls once stood—and the Paipais have held the area ever since. Although the mission is barely traceable, the cemetery where the missionaries were buried remains well preserved. The cemetery is also a Paipai graveyard and is considered sacred ground. You must have permission of the chief to visit or photograph it. He usually appears promptly from the bush to negotiate the fee.

Between Santa Catarina and Valle Trinidad the

narrow sand and clay road crosses a plateau of juniper and piñon pine, then becomes steep, rocky, and deeply eroded as it drops to Valle Trinidad. At the bottom of the hill you make a 45-degree turn to the left at the intersection. This wide dirt road is the main highway to San Felipe—and was once also the runway for the Valle Trinidad airfield (the old wind sock is flying on the left).

When it leaves the settlement of Valle Trinidad, the road crosses a level plateau and then begins the descent to sea level through San Matias Pass. After you pass a concrete gatehouse on the right and cross a cattle guard, you reach a branch road to the right; this road crosses the dry lakes and is 10 miles shorter to San Felipe, but it takes an hour longer—there's a sandy stretch before the dry lakes and a rocky stretch afterward that slows you down to five miles per hour. Continuing on the main road, you descend easily through a desert of chollas, *senitas*, ocotillos, elephant trees, and Mojave yuccas. There is excellent open camping all the way to Highway 5.

Sierra San Pedro Mártir

The most rugged of Baja's northern mountains is the Sierra San Pedro Mártir. Part of the range has been set aside as a wilderness area and is closed to hunting. Although there are no facilities of any kind, it has been designated as a national park. Several jagged peaks soar to heights of 9,600 feet or more; "El Diablo," the peninsula's highest mountain, has twin peaks of 10,152 and 10,156 feet. Backpacking, climbing, and trout fishing are popular; camping is permitted everywhere. The San Pedro Mártir is said to be the clearest spot on the North American continent. A new national astronomical observatory (now under construction and open to the public on a limited basis) is located on one of the peaks.

The sharply precipitous eastern side of the mountains must be reached on foot through canyons from the desert floor. The "dry lakes road" from San Felipe provides access to the canyons.

The western slope is reached from the west and north by a loop road that turns off the paved highway 9 miles south of Colnett and joins the Ensenada-San Felipe road 12.6 miles east of Valle Trinidad. This road leads to Meling Ranch and Mike's Sky Rancho, two guest ranches in the foothills of the San Pedro Mártir. Passenger cars do travel these roads all the time, but because of some steep, winding grades, vehicles with four-speed transmissions or four-wheel drive are preferred.

Meling Ranch is best approached from the Pacific coast highway. The preferred route to Mike's Sky Rancho is to turn off Highway 5, 30 miles north of San Felipe, and follow the Valle Trinidad road for about 36 miles. The turn to Mike's is well marked. Part of the last stretch to Mike's was cut through in 1970. It is flatter, straighter, and shorter than the previous route, which loops around it to the west. Both Meling Ranch and Mike's Sky Rancho are open all year; daytime temperatures in the winter are in the 60's.

The observatory can be reached by a poor logging road near Mike's Sky Rancho or by the better Socorro mine road from Meling Ranch. Although the roads meet, making possible a loop trip deep in the heart of the mountains, the logging road is so badly deteriorated it is nearly impassable. A new road to the observatory is under construction.

Meling Ranch. Whether you fly or drive, the first glimpse of Meling Ranch will be an aerial view of red roofs nestled among green cottonwoods. As the winding road crosses the last ridge top, a broad view of the San José Valley and ranch buildings below unfolds.

Also called Rancho San José, this 10,000-acre cattle ranch built by a pioneering family around the turn of the century is one of Baja's best-loved traditions. On your left as you approach is the rambling guest ranch that evokes nostalgia for an era of buckboards, crinolines, and warm Western hospitality. It is not entirely an illusion. The ranch offers civilized comforts while preserving many old-fash-

ioned customs. Meals are served family-style in a dining room warmed by a Franklin stove. Although there is electricity, the dining room and guest rooms are lit by coal oil lamps—guests demand them.

You can travel into the forested high country of the San Pedro Mártir on a guided pack trip from the ranch. The mountains are best in May, June, and early July. Winter snow (sometimes six feet deep) has melted, springs are overflowing, and the meadows are bright with wildflowers. A seven-day trip makes La Grulla Meadow a base camp for explorations. One side trip is to the site of the mission San Pedro Mártir; little remains except mounds of earth where rain has dissolved the mission's adobe walls, and the graves have been vandalized. In recent years Meling Ranch has been popular for one-week, 50-mile pack trips in mid-May sponsored by the Sierra Club (cost—$150). Special trips of almost any duration or length can be arranged directly through the ranch.

Saddle horses are available, and there is swimming in a stream-fed pool. At the present time no camping facilities are provided on ranch property.

For deer, mountain lion, and dove and quail hunting, guests must have a license and a gun permit. Only the license can be issued at the ranch. Hunting is not permitted within the national park.

Rates at the ranch are $30 per day for two adults, American plan, with a 10 per cent discount for seven days. Rates for children are $5, under 5 years; $7, 6 to 10; $10, 10 to 12. The ranch has short-wave radio transmitting and receiving facilities and can be reached via a phone patch. From the United States call 714-466-6872 or 213-790-4387 at 9 p.m. Pacific daylight saving time, 7 p.m. Pacific standard time. You can also call the ranch through Oscar Gonzales, ham operator in Ensenada, at Ruíz and Ninth Streets.

A private airstrip east of the ranch has an airport with tie-down facilities.

Mike's Sky Rancho. Mike's Sky Rancho is a guest ranch, not a working cattle ranch. The motel-type resort is built around a swimming pool and has modern accommodations. There is hunting for deer, wildcat, quail, and dove and fishing for rainbow trout in the San Rafael River that flows through the valley just below the ranch. The ranch will take hikers up to El Diablo and pick them up. Jeeps can be rented.

Rates are $15 per person per day, American plan, $95 per week. Developed campsites are provided along the trout stream. Facilities include lights, showers, and toilets. Camping fee is $5 for the first day, $3 each day thereafter.

An airport is located 6 miles south. Circle the resort to obtain transportation.

The Central Desert and

Gulf Coast

Wild Baja—great expanses of desert crossed by primitive roads—and picturesque towns beside the Sea of Cortez

SHARK *drying in the sun is common sight on the Cortez. Except for native fish camps like this and a few sport-fishing resorts, Baja coast is wild.*

THE WILD central desert of Baja, a ruggedly beautiful land of granite hills, lava plains, deep canyons, and long distances, is the least populated area of the peninsula. But if there are few people, the plant life is abundant, comprising one of the most remarkable collections of desert flora in the world. Over 100 species of cactus grow here, along with agaves, palo verdes, mesquites, elephant trees, and hundreds of other less conspicuous forms peculiarly adapted to survival in an arid environment.

In this desert the bizarre becomes the commonplace. Among the most striking plants frequently encountered are the *cardón*, the *cirio*, and the *Yucca valida*. The *cardón*, the tallest cactus in the world, grows everywhere in the central desert, sometimes reaching a height of 75 feet. The *Yucca valida*, a tree-sized yucca similar in profile to the Joshua tree, is scattered throughout most of the central peninsula, in places forming dense forests. The fantastic *cirio*, popularly called the "boojum," looks like no other plant in the world and grows only in the northern part of the desert.

The central desert of Baja, part of the Sonoran Desert, is subdivided into four principal regions. West of the peninsular range the northern half is called the Vizcaíno Region, the southern half the Magdalena Region. East of the peninsular range the northern half is an extension of the Colorado Desert, the southern half an extension of the mainland Gulf Coast Desert.

That the central desert remains largely unspoiled is due almost entirely to the bad roads in the northern half. There are no ribbons of concrete or asphalt crisscrossing the area, no power lines or billboards to mar the landscape. Except for a few primitive roads, some ranches, and a few missions (mostly in ruins), the northern half remains wild and undeveloped, and a trip through the region is a rugged road adventure.

In contrast, the southern half from Santa Rosalía to La Paz is developing rapidly and offers an entirely different type of travel experience. A wide road—much of it already paved—now follows the Gulf coast, connecting Santa Rosalía, Mulegé, and Loreto with La Paz. There are modern fly-in sport-fishing resorts at Loreto and Mulegé. Whether you come by plane or car, you have many options.

BUGGY competing in rugged "Mexican 500" rally races through boojum forest near Rancho Arenoso.

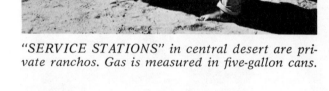

"SERVICE STATIONS" in central desert are private ranchos. Gas is measured in five-gallon cans.

You can visit missions little changed since Spanish times. There is magnificent game-fishing in the Gulf and excellent skin-diving and shell-fishing in Concepción Bay. Inland from the Gulf the desert is still wild and unexplored.

The most interesting way to see the central desert is to drive it. A road of sorts, full of chuckholes, ruts, and jagged rocks, winds through the northern half for nearly 400 miles before coming out at the Gulf at Santa Rosalía. Driving it is strictly for road adventurers, and no one should attempt it without the proper vehicle and adequate preparation (see page 7). There are two ways to approach from the north. The main highway comes down the Pacific coast from Ensenada and turns inland at El Rosario. The more difficult Gulf route bears inland at Gonzaga Bay and joins the main highway at El Crucero after 47 miles.

Both routes pass through interesting desert areas, and the main considerations favoring one over the other are the type of vehicle used and the season of the year. Because of the 20-mile stretch of steep, rocky road just below Puertecitos, only dune buggies, pickup trucks, and four-wheel-drive vehicles should attempt the Gulf route. In spring this is the best route for wildflowers, and the weather is ideal for camping out. But in summer, the Gulf coast becomes oppressively hot. Daytime temperatures soar from the 80's and 90's to 115

degrees when the wind shifts to the west.

The Pacific route, cooled in summer by ocean breezes and fog, has a poor road surface, too. There are miles of chuckholes and dips, but the sharp rocks on the other side of the Aguajito grade have been worn down by constant use, and some work has been done on the road. Any vehicle *can* get through now, but passenger cars are definitely not recommended. The Pacific route is the main highway and gets most of the through traffic traveling the peninsula.

If you drive the Pacific route, the adventure begins when you leave the dusty streets of El Rosario. The little agricultural settlement may not look like an outpost of civilization, but in retrospect it will seem so. For El Rosario is the last place for a couple of hundred miles offering groceries, tire repairs of a sort, gas from a pump, and telephone communications to the north.

A number of ranches along the main road between El Rosario and San Ignacio (the next town of any size) make this 337-mile stretch less isolated than it appears. At El Arco, about 75 miles northwest of San Ignacio, a small store sells a few supplies. Many of the ranches sell gas—when they have it. Hauled in by trucks in 50-gallon drums, it has to be siphoned into 5-gallon cans, then poured through a funnel into your gas tank. It's a good idea to bring a large chamois to stretch over the funnel to filter out any dust and water in the gas. If your gas gauge is getting low, don't bypass any ranch that has gas. The next ranch or town may have run out.

A few ranches serve simple meals when they are able to. Enchiladas, refried beans *(frijoles)*, tortillas, beer *(cerveza)*, and coffee are the usual fare. It is advisable to bring a camp stove and adequate provisions—in case your vehicle breaks down or meals are unobtainable.

Overnight accommodations and modern conveniences are nonexistent along the main highway, but there is excellent open camping everywhere. The whole central desert is a giant campground with few fences.

THE PACIFIC ROUTE

The dirt road from El Rosario turns inland, passing through irrigated farmland of the broad Arroyo del Rosario. After 6.5 miles, you reach an unmarked junction. (On the north side of the arroyo is El Castillo, a castlelike formation of rocks on the sheer cliff face.) The main road turns right and heads southeast. Straight ahead through the arroyo lies the Sauzalito mine road, which rejoins the main route west of Rancho Arenoso.

Both roads ascend a mountain, but the Sauzalito grade is spectacularly steep with sharp switchbacks and should be attempted only by vehicles with four-wheel drive or four-speed transmissions. The road is narrow, sometimes sandy, frequently rutty and rocky (with short stretches of exposed bedrock and sharp rocks on the side of the road). Nonetheless, it is the most scenic route in spring. There are magnificent views of the coastal mountains and Arroyo del Rosario, which looks like a miniature Grand Canyon in the distance. The road winds across narrow ridge tops, descends sharply into a wash-crossed valley, and near the inactive copper mine passes through a richly vegetated desert, outstanding for its varieties of large chollas. From March through May, along the lower, sandier stretches of desert, wildflowers are abundant.

Beyond the turnoff to the Sauzalito mine road, the main highway winds through a wide canyon over chuckholes and rutted tracks that send up swirls of dust. After a rain, the road becomes a sea of mud. The sage scrub of the Pacific coastal slopes gives way to desert vegetation. New kinds of chollas appear, with fuzzy, fingerlike arms, and you see an occasional cochal, a handsome tree cactus with thick clusters of clear-green branches that curve gracefully in the shape of a candelabra. In a few miles, what look like erratically placed, attenuated telephone poles turn up on the rims of the canyon. These are boojums, or *cirios*. Scattered

stands of boojums line the rest of this route south, becoming taller and assuming weird shapes around El Crucero, where they grow in forests.

After many a chuckhole, the road begins the Aguajito grade, passing a turquoise mine and ascending a series of switchbacks to nearly 2,000 feet. The ascent is relatively smooth over a gravelly surface with a few loose rocks, but the descent is sharp and rough and the roadbed filled with rocks. From the mountain summits on a fog-free day there are 180-degree views of the Pacific. After a steep switchback descent, the road traverses rolling tablelands through the granite mesa country of the interior. The altitude of 1,600 to 2,000 feet and the proximity of the Pacific make this desert unexpectedly cool. Although the days warm up, nights

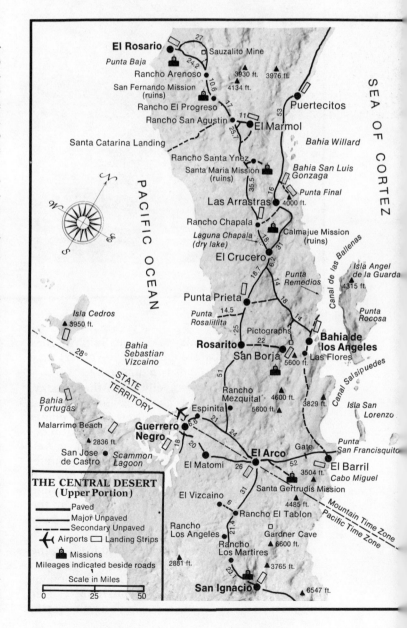

THE STRANGE BOOJUM

Of all the odd desert plants of Baja, the boojum is the most bizarre. Except for small stands near Puerto Libertad on the mainland and on Isla Angel de la Guarda, boojums grow only in an area about 250 miles long on the Baja peninsula. The tall trees, which resemble tapering telephone poles, are first seen below El Rosario. Farther south they grow in thick forests, below Rosarito they become sparse, and southeast of El Arco at Tres Vírgenes Volcanes they disappear altogether.

Mexicans call the tree *cirio* for its resemblance to a wax taper. The vernacular name "boojum" was bestowed by botanist Godfrey Sykes. When he first saw the tree he was reminded of the imaginary creature, called the Boojum, that dwelt on desert shores in Lewis Carroll's *The Hunting of the Snark*. A member of the ocotillo family, the tree has the scientific name *Idria columnaris*.

Young boojums start out as fat balls covered with long, thorny twigs. As they grow taller they look like inverted ice cream cones, then like parsnips. Some reach a height of 60 feet. Many boojums follow the straight and narrow, but others branch out in graceful or fantastic arches. A few loop to the ground and develop new roots.

In February and March, following winter rains, boojums are covered with dark green leaves which fade to yellow in spring and then drop, leaving a leafstalk that hardens into a sharp spine. The trunk stays bare until the next hard rain, when new leaves emerge above each spine. In late June and July, it sends forth small sprays of pale yellow flowers from the branch tips.

can be chilly, even in May and June. Summer fogs frequently roll in before dark, and the desert may be shrouded in mist until midmorning.

The road, sometimes gravelly, other times rocky, continues to wind over gently rolling hills and through rock-strewn arroyos. New desert plants appear—fleshy-leaved agaves, prickly pears (an occasional one simultaneously bearing orange, yellow, and salmon flowers), chollas with many spine-covered branches, and columnar *cardones*. In spring colorful clumps of yellow composites come into bloom. Bright splotches are provided by the little balls of red-spined barrel cacti, which bear burgundy-colored flowers in June.

At Rancho El Progreso, a sandy road leads to the right about 2 miles to the ruins of Mission San Fernando de Velicatá, the only Baja mission of Franciscan origin. It was founded in 1769 by Father Junípero Serra as he made his trek north to Alta

California. Only a few crumbling adobe walls remain, and there is a cemetery with headstones of more recent vintage. The mission ruins overlook a marshy arroyo filled with willows and reeds. Several families live nearby.

About 17 miles beyond El Progreso and a stone's throw before Rancho San Agustín is the turn southwest to Santa Catarina Landing on the Pacific, where blocks of onyx from El Mármol were once hauled by lighters to waiting ships. The road to the landing is poor and little-traveled. Beds of fossil ammonites, ancient relatives of the squid and octopus, are found a few miles from the coast. Fossilized specimens as large as two feet in diameter, resembling giant snails, have been dug out of the beds.

From Rancho San Agustín, you can take a rutty and rocky road that goes east to El Mármol, an onyx quarry that ceased operations in 1958. For nearly 60 years, tons of the varicolored, high-quality onyx were shipped to San Diego to be made into such things as inkwells and mantelpieces. Now the town is a ramshackle cluster of thatch-roofed houses, some with onyx foundations and walls. The most solid structures are the celebrated onyx schoolhouse and an onyx garage.

Beyond San Agustín, the countryside—and the road—gets rockier. Massive granite boulders of awesome size are strewn on the desert, some in solid isolation, others in great pyramids and piles. There are balancing rocks, rocks suggestive of animal shapes, and boulders bigger than houses. The road winds through rocky canyons on a surface that varies from rough bedrock to fine gravel. You frequently flush large coveys of quail, which are abundant the length of the peninsula wherever there is green plant cover.

You can fill up your water cans with good drinking water at the hospitable Rancho Santa Ynez, a working cattle ranch and a checkpoint for the Mexican 500 and 1,000 races. It has a landing strip. About 12 miles from the ranch is Mission Santa María, reached by a rough road. This was the last mission founded by the Jesuits before their expulsion from the peninsula. Only parts of the walls remain intact. At the ranch you can obtain directions to the mission.

Beyond Santa Ynez, the main road passes through sparsely vegetated desert. There is another steep, rocky grade and a stretch of giant boulders before the road drops into Laguna Chapala. For 4 miles before Rancho Chapala, you drive through a maze of deep silt and chuckholes, one of the dustiest areas in Baja and impassable after a deluge.

Rancho Chapala, one of the more developed ranches, is a principal stopping place for trucks and travelers making the peninsular journey. Simple meals can be obtained. There is usually gas. A 14-mile shortcut to the Gulf route, coming out near Las Arrastras, turns left here. Although used by racers in the Mexican 500, the road is poor.

Leaving the dusty, rutted tracks of Chapala, you soon reach the dry lake bed of Laguna Chapala. There is an exhilarating 2-mile ride across the crusty, hard-packed surface. When the ancient lake bed is dry (as it often is), it is a fine place to race a vehicle and also is a natural landing field. In winter, however, the lake bed may be under water, and vehicles have to find a path through the brush around the lake.

South of Laguna Chapala, the main road is flat, fast, and sandy through low brush country and jackrabbit flats. At nightfall, many long-tailed kangaroo rats can be seen in the beam from your headlights. The road changes to gravel, and the desert vegetation gets richer. Tall *cardones* appear, their fluted branches riddled with the nesting holes of the golden-headed Gila woodpeckers. Among the

striking desert plants are a kind of *candelilla*—clusters of green, leafless stalks tipped with red flowers in early spring—and fairy dusters with scarlet blossoms. Bushes of *chuparosa* bear red flowers that attract hummingbirds.

El Crucero, where the Pacific and Gulf coast routes join, is marked by a small adobe house where gas can be purchased from drums. To see one of the finest forests of boojums on the peninsula, make a short detour here and drive a few miles up the Gulf route.

THE GULF ROUTE

The moment you leave Puertecitos on a short, rocky rise, the road demands all your concentration. The next 20 miles is the worst stretch of any main route on the peninsula. For the first 10, it is alternately rocky and sandy as it climbs up and down low coastal hills, passing many lonely coves and crescent beaches that make perfect campsites. Long lines of pelicans skim over the surface of the sea. Along the coast you can find spiny murexes, prized by shell collectors; at low tide, when the offshore rocks are exposed, rock oysters can be gathered for a campfire supper.

For the second 10 miles, the road curves around and over the ridges of the volcanic coastal mountains, climbing a series of half a dozen rough, rocky grades, three of which are outstandingly steep. The surface of the road is consistently very poor, with deep ruts and sharp exposed bedrock. Deep in the canyons below the precipitous track lie the twisted wrecks of trucks and cars that have gone off the road.

When you can take your eyes off the road, the scenery is spectacular. From the ridge tops the deep-blue Gulf waters and the rugged coastal scarps stretch as far as you can see. From some heights, you may look down on crags topped with the nests of ospreys. These handsome fish-eating hawks have become increasingly rare in North America, but the wild seacoasts of Baja still ring with their piercing cries. Overhead an occasional frigate bird, the symbol of warm southern waters, glides and wheels on the rising thermals.

A simple concrete shrine marks the top of the last bad grade. Like all the roadside shrines in Baja, this one is dedicated to Our Lady of Guadalupe, the patroness of Mexico, and was erected by some traveler in return for having safely journeyed over the road.

There is a perceptible improvement in the road surface after the descent to sea level, but rough gravel, rocks, and some bumpy stretches make the rest of the trip to Bahía San Luis Gonzaga slow going. The road closely parallels the coast, passing a fish camp, and winds inland through a striking ocotillo desert. In mid-April, when the ocotillo comes into full bloom, the flowers cast a red haze to the horizon. In the rocky washes are smoke trees, palo verdes (a swarm of yellow flowers and bees in spring), and one of the most picturesque of Baja's desert flora—the elephant tree *(Pachycormus discolor)*, which grows the length of the central desert (see page 11).

Just before you reach Gonzaga Bay there is a dune-backed beach a couple of miles long that ter-

---

 THE FLOWERING DESERT

If you visit the arid central desert after a rainless summer or during one of the frequent periods of drought, the landscape is drab and gray. Bushes and trees are leafless and seemingly lifeless. But if you return after the winter rains have brought out green leaves, new shoots, and the first flowers, the desert looks very much alive with splashes of color everywhere.

As early as February the sandy desert stretches may be dotted with blue lupine, yellow poppies, purple sand verbena, and other shortlived wildflowers. In March, sometimes earlier, the wands of the ocotillo are tipped with scarlet flowers that last for many weeks. April is when the palo verdes are fragrant masses of yellow; mesquites and palo blanco trees have yellowish white or greenish flowers. In May the agaves send up their towering stalks of chrome-yellow blossoms. A bewildering variety of barrel cacti and chollas provide a succession of spring bloom and a dazzling display of colors—lime-green, rust, orange, red, and yellow. The desert, however, follows a calendar of its own. Mid-spring brings autumn for some trees. The green leaves that develop on *cirios* and elephant trees in early spring begin to glow with oranges and golds.

Summer brings another season of color. The creamy flowers of the tree yucca begin to bloom around June in the southern part of their range and in July in the north. In June and July, the elephant trees may be covered with sprays of delicate pink (sometimes yellow) flowers. The sweet and sour pitahayas blossom in late May and June, and their succulent crimson fruits, a staple of the Indian diet and still relished by the people of Baja, ripen in July and August.

The profusion and times of the flowering vary from area to area (the farther south, the earlier the bloom) and are governed by complex factors, such as adequate amounts of rain falling at the right intervals. In prolonged periods of drought, many of the plants remain leafless and don't bloom at all.

---

minates at a high lava headland. Good campsites protected from the wind can be found in the lee of the sand dunes.

On the shores of Bahía Willard and Bahía San Luis Gonzaga are two primitive fish camps, patronized chiefly by fly-in fishermen (each has an airstrip) and, in season, hunters after deer and the vanishing bighorn sheep. Both camps sell gas from drums, when they have it. There is no potable water in the area; the camps haul drinking water from Las Arrastras to the south. A new camp is under development just south of Gonzaga Bay.

On the scenic 47-mile stretch from the Gulf to El Crucero, you can cruise along at 20 to 25 miles per hour on the sandy or gravelly sections of the road, slowing to a crawl only for the few rough areas. In spring the sandy flats are covered with wildflowers in one of the most spectacular displays on the northern Gulf. The flowers generally burst into bloom in late February and early March but can begin as early as December.

A few miles before Las Arrastras, the roadbed gets bumpier as you ascend a picturesque boulder-strewn canyon filled with massive elephant trees and *torotes*. At Las Arrastras, an adobe by the side of the road, you can get drinking water from a well at the bottom of the arroyo behind the house. Goats come bounding down from the nearby hills, hoping for some spillover.

The long, broad valley of Calamajué stretches before you as you drive past wildflower flats and dip into washes shaded by spreading mesquites and palo verdes. The predominant plants are ocotillo, spiny chollas, and creosote bush. Just before descending into the gorge of Calamajué Canyon, look on the left for the ruins of mission Calamajué, founded in 1766. Only a portion of the foundation remains, barely discernible from the road. When the Jesuits discovered they couldn't grow crops in the canyon, they abandoned the site a few months after building the mission. On the steep slope below the mission is a gold ore mill.

The 8-mile drive up Calamajué Canyon follows the course of a small stream, crossing it many times, past sheer walls colorfully striated in ocher, turquoise, and white. Several palm trees grow in the canyon, and in the higher, damper reaches are thick stands of sedges and streamside shrubs. Near the top there is a pronounced change in the character of the vegetation. Strange boojum trees appear.

You climb out of the canyon into landscape that is a bizarre tangle of poles and balls and stiff-branched trees, bristling with thorns and tipped with daggers. The rich assortment of plants includes sour pitahayas, ocotillo, many varieties of chollas and barrel cacti, agaves, and tall *cardones* and tree yuccas. And everywhere there are boojums, some straight as a stick or looping gracefully to the ground, others standing on end like giant dinner forks. There are few places to turn off the road, but if you can find one, this fine boojum forest makes an interesting place to camp.

EL CRUCERO TO EL ARCO

The Pacific and Gulf routes join at El Crucero. On your way down the peninsula from here to El Arco you can take side trips to Bahía de los Angeles and its fishing resort, to the isolated community and mission of San Borja, and to Scammon Lagoon with its gray whales and salt-harvesting industry.

After 6 miles of fast road south from El Crucero, you come to the first turnoff to Bahía de los Angeles—a one-way side trip of 48 miles. (This is a much better road than the narrow, sandy, deeply rutted alternate route from Punta Prieta.) The main highway passes through forests of tree yuccas near Punta Prieta. There is usually gas available from drums at two places here. Below Punta Prieta there are long stretches of holes and dips.

Beyond Punta Prieta 7.3 miles, a side road at Rancho Bachandres goes to the Pacific, where lobster, abalone, and fish can be bought in season at Punta Rosalillita. South along the coast are some beautiful stretches of wild, sandy beach and many good campsites. In places the beach is strewn with iridescent wavy topshells and an occasional lobster trap. You may see schools of porpoises and sea lions offshore. This is not a quick jaunt from the main highway—there are many roads, and the one you are on may disappear entirely while crossing the top of some gravelly mesa. It is a trip for those with plenty of time and a good sense of direction.

At the tiny village of Rosarito, 25 miles south of Punta Prieta on the main road, you can buy gas, soft drinks, and beer. A side road turns off here to San Borja. Below Rosarito the road is downgrade —dusty, with a few holes, but good enough to drive a fast 20 or 30 miles per hour.

About 4 miles from Rancho Mezquital you pass a marked turnoff to Guerrero Negro and Scammon Lagoon, but there is a better road (not marked) 8 miles farther. (The side road forms a Y where it meets the main road, and in the triangle at the top of the Y is an old yucca fence.) From here on you cruise at an exhilarating clip through a forest of yuccas and giant *cardones* to El Arco.

Bahía de los Angeles

The fishing resort of Antero Díaz on beautiful Bahía de los Angeles is unique: It is the only place in

BARBECUED TURTLE is Baja specialty. Breast meat intact in shells is roasted before mesquite fire. Then the rich, oily meat is chopped and mixed with a chile-flavored tomato sauce.

THICK TRUNK, contorted branches, and pale papery bark distinguish the elephant tree.

the north central desert offering comfortable accommodations, good food, and showers (some with hot water), a luxury only the dust-covered desert driver can fully appreciate.

The road from the main highway to Los Angeles Bay is a scenic one through a *cirio*-covered desert, past an abandoned gold mine, and across a mountain range that affords panoramic views of the island-studded bay. It has a few rough stretches, but the first 14 miles are the smoothest since the dry lake bed of Chapala.

Turtles and tourists are the mainstay of Los Angeles Bay, a village with a permanent population of about 300. The *caguamas*, or green turtles, are diminishing from their former abundance. The tourists, however, are increasing, lured by good game-fishing, the unspoiled shoreline, and the beauty of the bay and offshore islands.

On the beach in front of Casa Díaz are the pens where the turtles, weighing up to 200 pounds, are kept in shade and water until trucks transport them north to Ensenada. The turtle fishermen hunt from canoes, using nets or harpoons, and may stay out 10 or 12 days at a time. In season some 150 to 200 turtles may be landed every month, a drop from previous turtle catches. To protect the dwindling green turtle fishery, the government has designated May through September a closed season—the time when turtles come close to shore and are easiest to find.

There are beautiful campsites up and down the beach, on the sandbar, and at La Gringa, but most visitors fly in to Los Angeles Bay and stay at Casa Díaz. At the busiest times (May and June and spring weekends and holidays) as many as 25 private planes may be lined up outside. When the 20 rooms are filled, the overflow sleeps on cots set up on the cabin porches or the beach. Everyone pays the same rate: $10 a day per person with meals, $5 without.

A few canned items and supplies are sold in the store adjacent to the dining room. There is good drinking water (free to campers) piped from a spring above the village. Automobile gas, usually available, costs a little more than on the main highway. Motorcycles ($4 an hour) and a pickup truck ($20 a day) can be rented.

In addition to a landing strip (with tie-down facilities) at the resort, there is a strip 3 miles south and an emergency strip 5 miles north for use in a crosswind. When landing at either of the latter, circle the resort several times first. Aviation gas is usually available.

The billfishes are uncommon this far north in the Gulf. But you can fish for sierra, cabrilla, grouper, yellowtail, and corvina in May and June. Dolphinfish turn up in late summer, and October is a good month for yellowtail. Four fishing boats, each with room for four people plus the skipper, are available for rent ($40 a day, gas extra). There are no small boats. The trawler *San Agustín* can be rented by parties of eight ($20 a day per person, three days minimum trip). A radiotelephone transmitter on the trawler makes it possible to telephone the United States from Casa Díaz via the high seas operator at Oakland, California.

At La Gringa, about 8 miles north of Casa Díaz, you can dig butter clams and get rock oysters. The shore teems with life—keyhole sand dollars, starfish, and pretty shells such as the pink murex. Lift a large stone at water's edge and you may even find an octopus lurking underneath.

Many islands dot the sheltered waters of Los Angeles Bay. Out in the Gulf, 45-mile-long Angel de la Guarda is a jagged silhouette with mountain peaks exceeding 3,000 feet. Its barren wastes are the home principally of such creatures as lizards and rattlesnakes.

An interesting pictograph site can be reached from the Los Angeles Bay road, 14 miles west of the bay. The turn, marked by a post but no sign, is an alternate route to San Borja. (As it is covered with sharp shale and receives little traffic, it is not recommended for reaching the mission settlement.) At 1.7 miles turn left. The road winds through dense thickets of oddly branching boojums, stately *cardones* and yuccas, and enormous bushy ocotillos. It is sandy, deeply rutted, and so narrow that you may have to hold back the unyielding limbs of *torote* trees, which leave an aromatic red stain and scratch the paint on your vehicle. Wildlife is abundant. Jackrabbits bound away in the brush and kit foxes are sometimes seen crossing the road.

At 6.2 miles you reach the pictographs, painted on and under overhanging rock ledges at the base of sheer vertical cliffs. Most are geometric designs or concentric circles in yellow, mustard, white, and orange. Almost as intriguing are the colorful lizards that dart in and out of crevices in the cliff. One large species sports a blue tail, black-and-beige striped body, olive head, and yellow chin.

San Borja

San Francisco de Borja is one of the three finest missions on the peninsula. To reach it, allow at least two hours one way. The mission is only 22 miles from Rosarito, but the road is rough, with sharp dips, and scattered with jagged rocks that can easily gash a sidewall.

Few visitors reach San Borja, and a new arrival is something of an event in the village. The children flock around, examining you and your belongings with a mixture of friendly curiosity and astonishment. As you explore the mission, they are your eager companions and guides, clambering up the belfry stairs and filling the empty church with echoes of laughter.

Set in a lonely canyon surrounded by lava mesas, the weathered mission church is constructed entirely of stone blocks, even to the vaulted roof. The church was finished by the Dominicans in 1801 and is complete save for a tower, which no one ever got around to building. The most impressive feature is the entranceway, flanked by two graceful pillars, with carved scrollwork around the

ISOLATED VILLAGE of San Borja has no priest. Children watch over the old stone mission.

arched door. The interior is benchless and almost bare. The simple altar is laid with dried flowers and drawings by the village children. A narrow circular staircase leads to the upper floor. The original mission bells, cast in Spain, have been stolen from the belfry. But, as the children will tell you, the bats *(murciélagos)* are still there, streaming out at dusk from the dark corners and chinks as they have for generations.

Adobe buildings and crumbling walls, the more impermanent remains of the Franciscan period, adjoin the church. Behind lies a graveyard that dates from the days of the Jesuits, who founded San Borja in 1759. The old burial crypts have been vandalized by treasure seekers.

Near the church are several mineral hot springs, an old Indian watering hole. The springs are the irrigation source for the village's gardens of dates, pomegranates, and olives. The village now consists of only a handful of families, who eke out an uncertain existence from the stony soil. But in the early days of the mission, some 3,000 Indians lived in this area. By 1818, when the last missionary left, epidemics had reduced the Indian population to less than 200.

Guerrero Negro and Scammon Lagoon

Guerrero Negro, the first community of any size after El Rosario, has the tempo of a bustling boom town. It belongs to Exportadora de Sal, a subsidiary of an American corporation, and is occupied exclusively with harvesting salt from the giant solar salt ponds along the shallow tidal flats.

The road from the main highway to the town, mostly sandy with a few ruts, passes through a barren desert broken only by scattered tree yuccas and jointed chollas. But in spring the sandy flats are covered with acres of wildflowers—daisies,

 WHALE WATCHING AT SCAMMON LAGOON

In January, February, and well into March, the surface of ordinarily placid Scammon Lagoon is broken by the blowing, barnacle-crusted hulks of gray whales. In a maneuver known as "breaching," the whales leap out of the water in an explosion of foam, or they "spy-hop" by lifting their heads straight up out of the water.

For the whales, Scammon Lagoon is a mating ground and maternity ward. Mating whales frequent the mouth of the lagoon and the breakers outside. The pregnant whales travel far into the lagoon to the quieter waters of the "Nursery." Here they give birth to one-ton calves which are 12 to 15 feet long. Human observers on shore can't see the births, which occur underwater, but one of the signs is the great flocks of gulls that gather to feast on the afterbirth. The mother and her calf are inseparable and stay in the lagoon for six to eight weeks before leaving for the Arctic. The babies are seen swimming alongside their mothers or atop their backs as they surface.

Every autumn, after summering in the plankton-rich polar waters of the northern Bering Sea, the gray whales begin their journey to their breeding grounds in Baja. It is a trip of 6,000 or more miles—possibly the longest migration of any mammal in the world—that is repeated when they return north in the spring. Traveling in small pods, the whales hug the coast on the migration south and can be spotted from many vantage points from British Columbia on down

the coast. The procession is spread out over many weeks. The whales parade by the whale-counting station at Point Loma in San Diego from December on. In January the lead whales reach Scammon Lagoon, where some 2,000 spend the winter. The rest push on hundreds of miles farther to San Ignacio Lagoon and the protected inlets near and in Magdalena Bay. A few round Cabo San Lucas and swim up the Gulf.

Between 6,000 and 7,000 gray whales may make this marathon migration each year, a remarkable comeback for a species that was brought to the brink of extinction by uncontrolled whaling. The wholesale slaughter began in the 1850's when Captain Charles M. Scammon stumbled upon the lagoon that now bears his name. Scammon was followed by hordes of whalers, who hunted the grays in all the estuaries of the Pacific coast. It wasn't until 1937, when no more than 100 grays were left, that the International Whaling Commission gave them protection.

For the few scientists and other whale watchers lucky enough to be at Scammon Lagoon (or at the less accessible lagoons along the coast) in the early months of the year, the whales are the greatest show in Baja. There are no tourist facilities of any kind at Guerrero Negro, the nearest town to Scammon Lagoon, but there are countless tracks through the underbrush to camping places on the beach. In winter, the weather can be cold, raw, and windy.

thick carpets of sand verbena, and clumps of a white-flowering ice plant. Along the road you'll see Harris hawks, one of the handsomest birds of prey, with striking black tails banded with white.

There are no overnight accommodations in Guerrero Negro. But you can replenish food supplies at several grocery stores which sell canned goods, fruits and vegetables, pasteurized milk, and eggs. All tap water in town is chlorinated and comes from company wells; it is safe to drink.

If you are interested in the salt-loading operation, drive to the principal salt pier. Here enormous trucks unload tons of salt through an iron gate in the roadbed, where a belt conveys it to a huge mountain of salt. Barges carry the glistening cargo to freighters at Cedros Island offshore.

The salt pier is also one of the places townspeople go to watch the gray whales in January, February, and March. In early morning and late afternoon the whales pass in and out of the mouth of the lagoon, spending the better part of the day in the ocean surf outside.

At Scammon Lagoon, about 18 miles from town, whale watchers have a panoramic view of the spouting, cavorting giants. The paved road to the lagoon leaves from the north side of town, passing miles of sparkling salt pans in whites, pinks, and pastels.

Many sandy roads lead to beaches on the lagoon. A few low dunes and hills provide partial protection from the wind, and some good campsites can be found. A dirt road to the right climbs a bluff, past some shacks, to a high vantage point for observing the gray whales. The tidal flats circling Scammon teem with shore birds, including avocets, stilts, and long-billed curlews.

Malarrimo or "Scavenger's Beach," a collecting basin for driftage washed in from all over the Pacific, can be reached by turning south at El Mátomi (20 miles east of Guerrero Negro) and driving around Scammon Lagoon. Almost waterless, this desert is one of the most treacherous on the peninsula. The trip to Malarrimo requires four-wheel drive and should be made in the company of at least one other vehicle.

El Arco

The mounds of whitewashed stones you see scattered on the slopes around the old mining town of El Arco are claim markers of hopeful prospectors. But now very little gold or ore of any kind is mined. About the only thing to see in town is the picturesque old gold-mining equipment in the arroyo behind the church. El Arco has no accommodations, but you can refuel and buy canned goods in the store.

MAGNIFICENT desert plants like these giant cardons are seen on San Francisquito road.

Just south of El Arco is the boundary between Baja Norte and Baja Sur—the state of Baja California and the territory of Baja California Sur.

San Francisquito and El Barril

A side trip northeast from El Arco takes you to San Francisquito, a beautiful bay of deep blue water lined with a crescent dune-backed beach. Once a pearling center, it is undeveloped except for a primitive landing strip in back of the beach. This spot is popular with fly-in campers, who can erect their tents within minutes of touching down.

El Barril, a private ranch, is several miles south on the Gulf coast. The ranch has its own landing strip (more than 2,000 feet long) and sells aviation gas (80 and 100 octane). Boats come in here for gas. When the Gulf waters are too rough, the ranch will truck gas to protected San Francisquito Bay. Good drinking water can be obtained at the ranch. Fish, turtle, and some vegetables can be bought when available.

The waters teem with sharks. In the spring of 1970, 425 sharks were caught in 27 hours by a net set close to shore at El Barril.

The road to the Gulf from El Arco is sandy and narrow but smooth driving for the first 30 miles. There are many clearings that make ideal camping spots. This road comes very close to being a dividing line between the four regions of the central desert, and it is one of the few places you can see almost all of the plants of the regions growing together. A forest of giant *cardones* in one section contains some of the tallest and finest specimens in Baja. The road crosses the top of the peninsular range through boulder-strewn hills studded with boojums.

Nearly 31 miles from El Arco, just before the descent to the Gulf, you reach an unlocked gate that serves as a drift fence for cattle. The grade beyond has a very poor surface. It is a good idea to park at the gate and walk down around the curve to see if anyone is climbing the hill. There are few turnoffs, and if you happened to meet an approaching vehicle it would be a difficult situation. As you descend, there are dramatic views of the distant Gulf, but these are eclipsed by more dramatic ones of the roadbed dropping away in front of your vehicle. In places near the top there doesn't seem to be any road at all. As your wheels on one side cross an outcropping of solid granite, the road on the other side drops off, causing your vehicle to pitch steeply. Crawling down with four-wheel drive in compound low, the tires slide a few inches down the sheer rock surfaces until they regain traction.

SOUTH TO SAN IGNACIO

Not all of Baja's dirt roads are bad, and the 75-mile stretch from El Arco to San Ignacio is one of the exceptions. It is basically hard-packed sand or adobe with only a few short stretches of bumps and dips. The first 20 miles or so after leaving El Arco are straight as an arrow—and fast.

For most of the trip you traverse a flat desert dominated by tree yuccas, in some places solitary sentinels and in others forming dense stands. You begin to see sweet pitahaya, the organ pipe cactus that will be a common sight as you travel farther south on the peninsula. In the latter part of May, elephant trees along this route start to send out sprays of dusty-pink flowers, and in June the yuccas begin to bloom.

YUCCA VALIDA resembles Joshua tree of Southwest. This forest is on main highway near El Arco.

El Vizcaíno, an agricultural settlement 6 miles from the main highway, has good water which can be obtained from any house with a garden hose. The turn, marked by a sign, comes about 31 miles south of El Arco.

At Rancho Los Angeles, a gas stop on the main road, you can have a soft drink or beer while you inspect a collection of arrowheads and metates.

Thirteen miles south of Rancho Los Angeles at Los Mártires, you can leave the main road and head south to Abreojos, a fishing camp on the Pacific. A side road from Los Mártires goes south 12 miles to San Angel, and here a road branches off 50 miles to Abreojos. This is an excellent place to see gray whales, buy lobster and abalone in season, and fish for corvina, *pargo*, and black sea bass. There is an airstrip.

By turning south at Los Mártires it is possible to take an alternate route down the Pacific coast via Cuarenta to La Paz. This sandy road is used by racers in the Mexican 1,000 and by through trucks.

Leaving Los Martires the road becomes gravelly and then very rocky approaching San Ignacio.

Indian rock paintings

Deep in inaccessible canyons in the Sierra San Francisco east of Rancho El Tablón, spectacular

SAN IGNACIO'S fine old mission faces shady plaza. Oasis village is verdant with date palms and fruits.

INGENIOUS WINDMILL was constructed from old auto parts. In Baja nothing goes to waste.

Indian paintings dating back to the early 1400's have been found on rock shelters. It has been estimated that there are at least 100 sites extending over a distance of 100 miles. The paintings, elaborately done in whites, blacks, and reds, are very sophisticated depictions—life-size and larger —of human and animal figures.

Several of the caves were discovered by Leon Diguet prior to 1895; the Spanish knew of the existence of such rock paintings more than a century earlier. The most publicized site, known as Gardner Cave, was found by writer Erle Stanley Gardner on a helicopter exploration in 1962.

San Ignacio

Coming upon the luxuriant greenness of San Ignacio after hundreds of miles of hard, dusty driving, you feel like the classic desert straggler who has seen mirages around every arroyo and doesn't believe his eyes when he comes upon a spring of fresh water. San Ignacio occupies the site of the old Indian *ranchería* of *Kadakaamang*— "arroyo of the carrizal"—named for its reed-lined pools and springs that bring water to this arid area of volcanic rock. Several springs, now impounded for irrigation, nurture some 80,000 date palms,

nearly two thousand orange trees, and many other fruits, including grapes which some villagers make into a robust wine.

San Ignacio gets every traveler's vote as the most charming oasis on the peninsula. The streets are narrow, crooked, and hilly, the thatched adobe houses picturesque and colorful. Bright pink benches circle the laurel-shaded plaza; in the center of the plaza stands a mustard-yellow fountain. The village houses are paint-splashed in reds, yellows, and blues. Yards are filled with bougainvillea, hibiscus, and flowering trees. Gardens are profuse with bananas, papayas, blackberries, and green and purple figs—the sweetest figs anywhere.

The village has, besides, one of the finest examples of mission architecture on the peninsula. The solid lava-block structure (its walls are four feet thick), founded by the Jesuits in 1728 and later finished by the Dominicans, is remarkably well preserved. Especially notable are its ornately carved doors and stone details. The interior has a soaring, arched ceiling. Peering down from the corners are tiny stone angels. The simplicity of the cool and tranquil interior reveals a sensitivity to the natural beauty of stonework and reflects the care the villagers have given their mission. The most significant restoration in recent times involved removing the repeated plasterings that had buried the original framework of the walls. A decade ago, the priest laboriously scraped away the accumulated

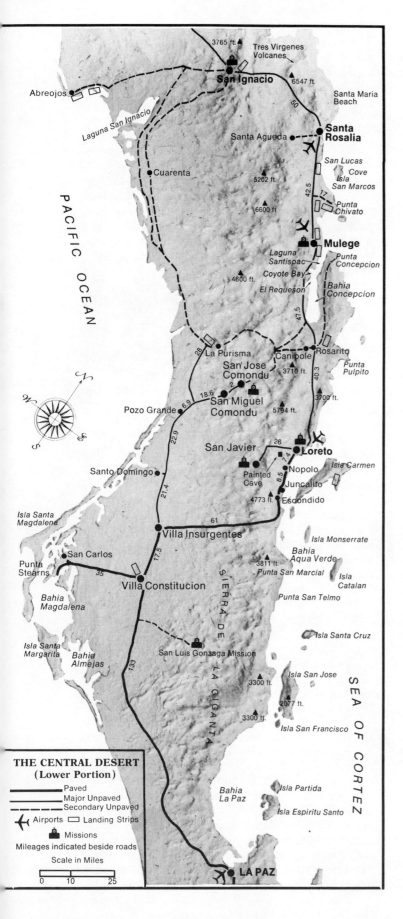

THE CENTRAL DESERT
(Lower Portion)

— Paved
— Major Unpaved
--- Secondary Unpaved
✈ Airports ▢ Landing Strips
🏛 Missions
Mileages indicated beside roads
Scale in Miles

0   10   25

crusts of the years to expose the natural tan stone frames around the windows, arches, and recesses. His successor has continued the gargantuan job, restoring the baptistery (on the right as you enter the church).

The coolest place in town is the grove of date palms, started by the Jesuits shortly after the mission site was established. Driving through the grove, you pass the racks where bunches of dates are spread out on mats to dry. The fruits are harvested in the autumn months when they are yellow and semi-ripe. Some trees have two fruitings a year and produce clusters in late spring. Many trees are badly charred from a fire that swept through the grove in 1970.

A monument to Mexican ingenuity and a local curiosity is a windmill on the road to Santa Rosalía. Built entirely of old automobile parts, it was created by a former mayor of the village.

The area around San Ignacio is rich in Indian remains. In the mountains northeast of town is the spectacular Serpent Cave mentioned in the writings of Erle Stanley Gardner. Just to reach the cave requires a full-day trip on burro. Arrangements for guides and provisions can be made through Frank Fischer of San Ignacio, who discovered the cave while on a hunting trip. Fischer is something of a Baja legend. A German, he came to San Ignacio in 1910, and his auto repair and welding shop has doctored many ailing vehicles making the trek down the peninsula.

Only two places in San Ignacio offer accommodations and meals. One is Casa Leree, just a block from the plaza. It presents a solid adobe wall to the street, but you enter into a spacious inner court shaded with a monumental grapevine. A gurgling stream, used for utility water, runs right through the courtyard. Accommodations are limited to two rooms and two dormitories, but extra cots are put up for large groups. The rates are $5 a day for room and board. In game season, venison and quail with wine are specialties.

At the Oasis (on the highway leading to El Arco) palm-thatch shelters for motorcyclists and campers have long-legged canvas cots for beds (50 cents). A separate building contains hot-water showers; for a small fee, you can stop and wash off the accumulated dust of several days' driving. The Oasis restaurant serves good, simple food. During the winter and spring months, you are treated to Pacific lobster, served in tacos or as a sauté with vegetables and chile.

There are several grocery stores in town, and a bakery located in one of the school buildings turns out excellent crusty *bolillas* and *pan dulce*.

No airlines stop at San Ignacio, but there are three landing strips for light planes near town. Taxis make frequent trips to Santa Rosalía.

THE GULF COAST

The road from San Ignacio to the Gulf coast passes through lava rock country, in places a profusion of desert plants. Rising dramatically from the plains are three conspicuous volcanic peaks—Las Tres Virgenes—which last erupted in 1790. One, Santa Barbara, is still warm and deposits hot water and sulphur in a nearby arroyo.

In the flat valleys, the road is an easy-to-drive hard dirt surface. But wherever there is a slight rise, the going gets rough; in a few stretches you drive over a staircase of rocks. The most memorable part of the trip, however, is not the rocky road but two spectacular mountain grades. Both are steep and have many sharp hairpin curves. You may have to back up to get around some of these. There are few turnoffs on the narrow grades. But both have been improved in recent years; rocks have been built up to widen the most precarious switchbacks. As a San Ignacio resident said, "Only a few trucks go over the side now."

The first grade, Cuesta de las Vírgenes, begins about 25 miles from San Ignacio. Several miles after the descent you reach a rocky plateau where suddenly there is a sweeping view of the Gulf and, a thousand feet below, the desert floor. Before you realize it you've started to descend the Cuesta del Infiernillo—the "grade to hell"—a tortuous journey of 2 miles. At the bottom is a wide arroyo and soon afterward the Gulf. To the left a shore road leads to Santa María beach, a sheltered cove popular with campers and surf fishermen.

Santa Rosalía

Santa Rosalía is unlike any other place in Baja. The creaky wood-frame buildings with their old-fashioned verandas look more like a stage set for the Old West than Old Mexico. A French mining company originally built the whole place around the turn of the century, importing everyone and everything, including the green prefabricated iron church. They later abandoned it to the Mexicans, but the town remains partly French. Some of the old buildings, still in use, are almost museum pieces. You can easily spend several days poking around the ancient mining equipment, but some things can be seen simply by driving around town: the old smelters, the office building built on the hill in 1893, and the donkey engines that hauled ore down from the mines on narrow gauge tracks.

Swing by the waterfront and see the unusual harbor. The principal attraction is the shipwrecked *Santo Domingo*, right in the middle of everything on the beach. Of more interest to boats entering the harbor are the hulls of ships which lie beneath the surface, unmarked. Just south of the harbor there is a public beach that is unique on the peninsula. Slag dumped offshore has washed in and turned the sand black.

CUESTA DE LAS VIRGENES between San Ignacio and Santa Rosalia descends a series of switchbacks.

There is fishing in the Gulf for grouper, corvina, red snapper, sierra, and roosterfish.

Santa Agueda makes an interesting side trip. This tiny oasis in the hills 10 miles south of Santa Rosalía grows papayas, mangoes, dates, bananas, and figs. Santa Rosalía's excellent water is piped from Santa Agueda springs.

Where to stay. Hotel El Morro, 1 mile south of town, will be the only place in Santa Rosalía offering modern accommodation. The dining room will specialize in French and Mexican-American food.

Hotel Francis, on the hill north of town, primarily serves the mining company but takes other guests, too. Hotel Central is located in town near the church. The Central's rooms are on the second floor above its bar, pool hall, and dining room.

Transportation. Aeronaves de Mexico flies daily to Santa Rosalía. Planes are met by taxis at the airport on the hill just south of town. The field at San Lucas Cove is no longer used for passenger flights.

Ferry service is planned between Guaymas and Santa Rosalía.

Below Santa Rosalía

Beginning at Santa Rosalía, a wide graded road now extends all the way to Villa Insurgentes, where

SANTA ROSALIA'S BAKERY

A visit to the renowned *panadería* of Santa Rosalía is one of the high points of a trip down the peninsula. The bakery dates from the city's French days, and everything is baked in mesquite-fired brick ovens which were built in 1903. Every day the bakery makes a tempting variety of sweet and plain rolls.

The photograph shows a sampling of the baked goods offered. The tray on the left holds an assortment of *pan dulces: quequitos* (cupcakes),

elotes (ears of corn), *campachanas* (puff pastries), *roscas* (rings), sweet *empanadas* filled with guava paste, *trenzas* (braids), and *cuernos* (horns). On the tray on the right are plain rolls, some with untranslatable names: *conchas chocolates* and *conchas blancas* (cocoa and plain shells), a *lima* (lime), a *cuadrito* (crisscrossed on top), *virginias* (unpatterned rolls), long *bolillas* (crusty rolls), and *pitahayas* (simulating the pitahaya fruit half peeled).

YOUNG SKIN DIVERS learn how to use scuba gear in the safety of the Punta Chivato pool. Many resorts rent diving equipment, several have instructors.

it connects with the paved La Paz highway. Part of the way the road is "washboard." The Mexicans, with characteristic humor, call it *"permanente,"* comparing it to a woman's waved hair. After a few miles, every part of your vehicle seems to be coming loose. The surface is covered with gravel, and a vehicle passing at even moderate speed can send a stone through your window. In mid-1971 only the section of the road between Mulegé and Loreto remained unpaved.

San Lucas Cove, a long, shallow lagoon about 10 miles south of Santa Rosalía, is bordered by graceful palm trees which provide many secluded beach campsites. The sand and mud flats of the cove are excellent for clamming—and have been for centuries. The largest Indian shell mounds on the peninsula line the shore in back of the beach.

Farther down on the Gulf coast is Hotel Punta Chivato, a well-equipped fly-in sport-fishing resort on the end of the rocky point of land for which it is named. The resort's handsome, modern design makes lavish use of stone and Guadalajara tile. Rates (American plan only) are $30 and $40 a day double. In addition to its own fleet of 28-foot sport-fishing cruisers, the resort has complete diving equipment and the services of a full-time instructor. There is good diving for scallops, giant clams, and lobster in season and for many kinds of fish offshore and at nearby islands. Two airstrips are adjacent; fuel is sold at one when available.

The Punta Chivato resort can be reached by a dusty road that leaves the main highway 25 miles south of Santa Rosalía. The turn is marked by several whitewashed rocks.

Mulegé

An enchanting river lined with date palms and orchards of papayas and mangoes gives the little oasis of Mulegé tropical languor and beauty. From the dirt paths that wind along the riverbank, you see an occasional skiff gliding over the placid waters. At the river's mouth is a landmark well known to mariners: El Sombrerito, a sombrero-shaped hill topped with a lighthouse. Two miles upstream sits the pretty little village of thatched adobes and gardens of flowers and tropical fruits. A mile above the village the river is dammed, attracting dozens of wheeling and diving frigate birds. Here, Mulegé's fortresslike mission commands a high overlook with a sweeping view of the village and the river as it disappears in a jungle of palms.

Located near the mouth of beautiful Concepción Bay, Mulegé is ideally situated for skin-diving and shell-fishing trips to the bay and game-fishing in Gulf waters. On the edge of town two modern resorts with airstrips have charter boats ready to whisk fly-in sportsmen to the best fishing grounds.

BURRO ambling along river road bears large roost-erfish, a gift from a Mulegé sport-fishing boat.

LA CHAYO sells Mexican folk art and crafts, displays Castaldí Collection of Baja Indian artifacts.

The village itself is a picturesque maze of winding streets barely wide enough for burro and pedestrian traffic and a tight squeeze for automobiles. At times the streets hum with activity. Burros loaded with bundles of firewood plod up the hills. In late afternoon when the water is turned on, the few street faucets become gathering places for villagers, who exchange a little gossip while filling buckets and pails. You may see a boy going from house to house, selling steaming-hot beef tamales tied in corn husks. Or you may happen on a vendor offering Mexican popsicles made with fresh fruits like watermelon and pineapple.

What to see and do. A boat trip is the best way to see Mulegé's junglelike river, which suggests a scene from the movie *The African Queen.* Along the banks of Rio Mulegé (Rio Santa Rosalía de Mulegé) are mangrove thickets, the underwater hiding places of the elusive snook, and clumps of carrizo, the reed villagers weave into mats and walls for their houses. Birdlife is abundant—mergansers and ducks frequent the river at the mouth, green herons fish along the banks, and hooded orioles are a splash of orange in the riverside trees.

The narrow river roads are natural paths for horseback and burro rides. Boats, burros, and horses can be hired through the resorts.

The Mission Santa Rosalía de Mulegé, upstream from the village, is a massive lava rock structure built in 1766. A rocky promontory behind the mission affords excellent views of the river.

Often mistaken for the mission, the territorial prison for Baja Sur is on a hill directly in back of town. Prisoners are permitted to leave during the day but must return at night. A guard still occasionally sounds a conch shell to summon back prisoners in the evening, but this practice is falling into disuse.

Spectacular cave paintings in the hills west of Mulegé take a day to reach, and you need a guide. The trip costs about $20. For information, check with any resort or with Harrison Evans at La Chayo gift shop.

In the estuary and near shore you can fish for yellowtail, grouper, roosterfish, cabrilla, sierra, bonefish, corvina, snapper, giant pompano, bonito, and skipjack. Snook are speared in the river from December to February. They are not fished by hook and line, and few are taken. Marlin, sailfish, dolphin, and other game fish are caught around islands nearby. The resorts can also arrange fishing, skin-diving, and shell-fishing excursions to Concepción Bay.

Castaldí collection. A great deal of archaeological material relating to the Indian pre-history of Baja California is either in private hands or in museums and universities. But the famous "Castaldí Collection," the largest collection of aboriginal artifacts on the peninsula, is on public display at La Chayo gift shop in Mulegé. Padre César Castaldí, S.J., priest of the mission at Mulegé from 1905 to 1946, assembled the artifacts. Most were given to him by ranchers in the Mulegé area, and the collection has been expanded with other archaeological materials from all over the peninsula.

Shopping. Nancy's and La Chayo are two tasteful gift shops in the village, with good crafts gathered from all over Mexico. At the thatch-roofed La Chayo, for example, you can shop for wooden salad bowls from Michoacán, Tonalá pottery, colorful handwoven bedspreads, tablecloths, napkins, hand-embroidered dresses from Guadalajara, and embroidered blouses and scarf dresses designed and made by the owner's wife.

A new addition to the village plaza is the modern Super Mercado Real, the best-stocked market between Ensenada and La Paz.

Where to stay. A sign outside a 200-year-old adobe near the plaza reads: "Vieja Hacienda Hotel—Broken English spoken." Inside the Hacienda Hotel, a spacious courtyard lined with rocking chairs is filled with colorful bougainvillea, including one purple-flowered specimen 90 years old. The rooms are enormous, with high beamed ceilings and adobe walls three feet thick. Rates are $10 a day per person on the American plan, $5 on the European plan. The owner, incidentally, speaks excellent English.

El Marisol, on a hill overlooking the Gulf and the boat harbor, is Mulegé's newest resort. The accommodations are attractive, native-style cabanas thatched with palm fronds. The cuisine is sophisticated and includes continental, American, and Mexican dishes. Rates are $12.50 per person per day, American plan. Meals are served only to guests.

Hotel Mulegé, formerly Club Aero Mulegé, changed its name when it changed owners in 1966. Mulegé's most deluxe resort, the hotel has luxurious rooms opening onto gleaming tiled walks draped with bougainvillea ($22 a day per person, American plan; $35 double). The resort has its own airstrip and will arrange fishing, hunting, skin-diving, and sightseeing excursions for its guests. Cruisers are $60 a day. The resort will serve meals to non-guests.

Serenidad Mulegé is a fly-in resort situated on the south bank of the river at its mouth. You have a choice between native-style cabanas (for four or eight persons) at $12 a day per person and individual cottages at $16 a day per person. Accommodations are American plan only. Non-guests can have meals here but should give an hour's notice. The resort has its own fleet of outboards and cabin

UPSTREAM, Mulegé's lazy river disappears into a jungle of palms. View is from bridge.

cruisers ($35 to $60 a day) and also rents river canoes ($2 an hour).

Las Casitas hotel in the village charges about $10 a day for a single, $20 for a double room.

Transportation. Aeronaves de Mexico makes regularly scheduled flights to Mulegé. Planes land at Chavez strip 5 miles west of town.

Concepción Bay

Nothing you've read or heard will quite prepare you for the spectacular beauty of 25-mile-long Concepción Bay, the gem of the Baja peninsula. Every curve of the shoreline brings a new discovery—a hidden cove, a mangrove lagoon, a crescent beach sparkling with white sand, a cactus-covered mountain slope. The bay waters, incredibly blue in the depths, turn to shades of turquoise and green in the shallows; at sunset water, sky, and mountains all look as if you were viewing them through red glasses. The water is so clear that you don't need goggles or a face mask to see beneath the surface. On a calm day you can stand on shore and watch exotically colored fish swimming in this natural aquarium.

There are many lonely coves and beaches where you can put up a tent or unroll a sleeping bag and have only burros and shorebirds as companions. Summer is hot on the Gulf, but the rest of the year is balmy—in December and January daytime temperatures will be in the mid-60's, nighttime temperatures in the 40's.

The bay is no longer quite as isolated as it once was. The new graded road provides quick access to the entire western shore of the bay. Some of the old road remains, and for those who have the time it is a more scenic stretch.

Much of the shoreline is now in private hands, and residents of Mulegé predict the bay will eventually become another Acapulco. But at present it is unfenced and unposted, and you will see nothing on the shores except an occasional fish camp.

Laguna Santispac, one of the most popular spots on Concepción Bay, is a lovely sheltered cove with sandy beaches and mangrove inlets. Located nearly 14 miles south of Mulegé, it has long been known for the succulent butter clams burrowed in the muddy bottom. Santispac still has clams, but not in the abundance of yesteryear—too many clam diggers have left their tracks in the mud. But in the less-visited flats and coves nearby you can find plenty of butter clams and large brown *chocolates* (pronounced cha-co-LAH-tays) to steam for supper. The same is true for the "oysters that grow on trees." Many of the oysters left on the mangrove roots at Santispac are clusters of empty shells, but live ones abound in other mangrove inlets. After half an hour and a cut finger or two, you can fill a bucket. Extracting the thumbnail-sized morsels will take the better part of another hour, and all you'll have for your efforts is about a third of a cup of oysters. They are sweet tasting, but other shellfish produce a heartier meal.

The large pen or fan shell, regarded highly by the Mexicans, has meat that resembles a scallop in taste and texture. Pen shells are usually obtained by diving, but at low tide if you wade out into water about two feet deep you may trip over one in the sand. An average shell a foot long and five inches wide will provide enough meat for two generous servings. Open the shell and remove the white muscle. Eat it raw, as the fishermen do, or marinate it

for an hour or two in lime juice with onions and chiles for a *seviche*. Cooking may make the pen-shell meat tough and indigestible.

Below Santispac is protected Coyote Bay, where shrimp boats and private yachts find shelter behind the islands in rough weather. The beaches are favorites with campers, particularly the most southerly one, shaded with mesquites and a cluster of tall palms. The rocky bluff at the end of the beach is a good place to fish or just fish-watch.

El Requeson, an idyllic cove beyond Coyote Bay, is named for the island connected to the beach at low tide by a sandbar. There are many good camping spots on the beaches. South of El Requeson and at other places along Concepción Bay, pelicans (usually in early evening) put on some of the best shows in Baja. When predators have driven a school of fish to the surface, as many as a hundred pelicans will plunge into the fray and gorge themselves on the easy prey. Also on hand may be a few frigate birds—the pirates of the sea—which gang up on the pelicans and try to pilfer fish from their pouches.

AT SUNRISE over the still waters of Concepción Bay, the only sound may be the distant hum of a shrimp boat. Sheltered coves like this one at El Requeson make ideal camping spots.

Concepción Bay is separated from the Gulf by a long, mountainous peninsula with many beautiful coves and unspoiled beaches. Except for an isolated fish camp or two, this peninsula is completely wild and seldom visited. A dirt road follows the shore on the bay side almost to Point Concepción at the peninsula's tip.

Loreto

Loreto could be a travel advertisement for a South Pacific island paradise. Its tall, arching date palms extend back from the beach, creating a cool canopy over the village's thatched adobes. At sunrise the palms are silhouettes against the pink-streaked sky. And although the town isn't really a jungle of tropical growth, in places the profusion of greenery and bright-flowered flame trees is strongly suggestive of one. Life here is easygoing, and activities center around the sea and the shore.

Most of the glamorous game fish of the Cortez —marlin, sailfish, dolphinfish, yellowtail, roosterfish, sierra, yellowfin tuna, amberjack, and many others—are caught in nearby waters. Large grouper frequent the reef at the northeastern end of mountainous Isla de Carmen. In winter smaller fish of many of the same species can be caught from shore so easily it's hardly a contest. From October through February, the townspeople rise before dawn and head for the beach and town pier to fish. In a half hour's time they're likely to pull in eight or more sierras and small yellowtails and roosterfish. Then the children go off to school, the fathers to work.

In season there is good hunting for white-winged dove and quail and, in the Sierra de la Giganta, for deer and mountain lion. Guns are not available at the resorts, but licenses can be obtained in Loreto.

A stroll through town can include a visit to the "Mother of Missions," whose blue-paneled, domed tower is visible from several miles away. The first in a chain of missions that eventually extended all the way into the present state of California, the church wasn't completed until 1752, 55 years after the Jesuits made Loreto the first permanent Spanish settlement on the peninsula. The church has

PALMS provide the romantic motif of the Oasis, a hospitable hacienda in a South Seas setting.

MOTHER OF MISSIONS, where it all began, is Loreto. From here padres explored the peninsula, establishing missions in both Californias.

GREAT GAME-FISHING in Gulf waters is only minutes away from private pier of Flying Sportsmen Lodge.

been damaged by earthquakes and restored and rebuilt many times.

Stop at Loreto's bakery, between the plaza and the beach. You hear the clear whistles of caged cardinals and the croaking of parrots on several streets in town, but the baker's yard is a noisy and colorful menagerie of iguanas, badgers, mockingbirds, cardinals, white-winged doves, turkeys, and ducks. Inquire when the baker plans to make his next batch of *pan dulce* in the large outdoor beehive oven. It is a treat to watch the trays of sweet rolls go in, then five minutes later emerge golden-brown, and to taste them hot and freshly baked. What you won't see is the labor involved in baking bread the old way. The baker will have been up since 4 a.m. making and shaping the dough, firing the oven with creosote bush and *palo de arco* woods, removing the coals, and throwing water inside the beehive to create the hot steam for baking.

It is a short walk from the bakery to the cement *malecón* lining Loreto's waterfront and the new pier, dedicated in 1969. Every week freighters from Guaymas, loaded with produce, anchor offshore. Local *canoas* are paddled out to pick up the cargoes, which are unloaded on the beach beyond the pier.

Where to stay. Although Loreto is a small town, it offers a choice of places to stay. The three principal resorts are all on the beach and have unobstructed views of the Gulf. The Hotel Oasis, set in attractively landscaped grounds of flowers and palms, combines Mexican warmth, hospitality, and atmosphere with modern comforts. Rooms in the ranch-style resort are off a long, palm-thatched veranda. The cuisine is excellent; homemade fruit pies and Mexican specialties are offered. Rates (American plan only) are $10 and $12.50 a day per person, $20 and $25 double, $27 for three in triple room. Meals also are served to people not staying at the resort. Fiberglass sport-fishing boats (made on the premises, and capable of speeds up to 40 miles per hour) are $55 per day for four. The Oasis is closed annually from July 15 to September 30.

The American-style Flying Sportsmen Lodge, on the beach south of the Oasis, is also a garden spot of flowers and shade trees. A friendly, relaxed fishing resort, the Lodge offers attractive accommodations (with up-to-date conveniences) in bungalows with marine views. The main lodge is built partly around a large swimming pool. The dining room features a variety of seafood, including barbecued turtle. The lodge has its own pier. Rates (American plan only) are $15 a day per person, $25 double. Sport-fishing boats are $25 a day for the smaller ones, $65 for larger boats that accommodate six.

The new Hotel Misión de Loreto, on the beach near the town pier, is a deluxe two-story hotel.

At Calle Salvatierra 3, in town almost opposite the church, the guesthouse of Doña Blanca de Garayzar has rooms with private bath. A bougainvillea-shaded patio and garden at the rear is filled with flowers and caged songbirds. Room and board is $5, and room only is $2. Señor Garayzar grows grapes at his Rancho Zacatel outside Loreto and makes a good dry white wine and a surprisingly smooth brandy, using old stills and equipment. You can buy the wine and brandy at the guest house.

Transportation. Aeronaves de Mexico makes daily flights to Loreto. The municipal airport is half a mile north of town.

San Javier

No road on the peninsula offers more scenic views of plunging cliffs and palm-filled canyons than the 26-mile drive southwest from Loreto to San Javier, with its 200-year-old mission. The road makes a switchback ascent through a cut in the Sierra de la Giganta.

About 6 miles from the main highway, you reach the beginning of the canyon drive. Narrow and rocky on the short, steep grade, the road follows and frequently crosses a winding stream where still pools reflect towering fan palms. Enormous *zalates*, or wild fig trees, grow along the banks. The trees produce tan, sweet-sour fruits which ripen in summer. The canyon is filled with birdsong and wildlife. Several species of hummingbirds dart across the stream, hovering for a moment to drink. The streak of purple is the Costa's. The feathery comet that flashes rufous and green is the Xantus, a hummingbird found only in Baja. It has a black-tipped red bill.

Near the beginning of the canyon drive (almost 8 miles from the main highway), you reach the "Painted Cave of Loreto," which has a small number of Indian paintings. The "cave," a shallow rock shelter at the base of cliffs, is in the arroyo on the left side of the road. Landmarks for this unmarked site are a hill just after the arroyo and the remains of a stone corral not easily seen from the main road. (If you pass an abandoned ranch with a corral, you have overshot by half a mile.) To reach the pictographs you walk past a grove of mesquites and follow the stream a short distance.

Farther up the canyon you pass Rancho las Parras, where you can buy sweet lemons and sour oranges. The oranges, the size of grapefruits, have thick, loose-fitting skins and a tart but refreshing taste. The ranch cures olives in cowhide vats just below the ranchhouse. Other fruits grown along the stream include mangoes, figs, and dates.

Your first impression of San Javier may be the sounds of tinkling bells and bleating goats. Goats are about the noisiest and most numerous inhabitants of this appealing little village. The main—and only—street is lined with a neat row of whitewashed, thatched-roof adobes and ends at the massive mission, built at the base of a black lava cliff. Arrive on a Saturday morning and several local musicians may be practicing inside the mission church, the strains of a squeaky violin and the softer chords of a guitar drifting out into the still and dusty street. A group of boys in the mission courtyard groan when the violinist hits a high note. A few black-garbed women enter the church, a boy on a burro ambles past, and the height of excitement comes when a furiously barking dog chases a steer down the street.

The memorable mission, known as San Francisco Javier de Vigge, stands essentially unchanged since it was completed in 1758. Constructed of blocks of rock cut from the lava hills of the countryside, it has endured two centuries and is the best preserved in Baja. It has also largely escaped the depredations of vandals who have looted most of Baja's missions. The resplendent gold-encrusted altar is still intact. Climb the spiral staircase to the loft and bell tower for a good view of the town.

Oranges and pomegranates grow in the mission courtyard. And the old mission garden nearby, now the property of various villagers, still produces dates, citrus, figs, and grapes. Several venerable olive trees with gnarled multiple trunks are said to have been planted by the early padres.

The villagers are proud of their handsome mission, but they point with almost as much pride to their small electric plant, gaily painted with reds and blues and nearly obscured by hollyhocks. San Javier has been electrified since 1969.

LORETO TO LA PAZ

About 7 miles after the road from Loreto joins the main highway you come to the hidden cove of Nopoló. Herons and egrets stand motionless in the mangrove *estero* you pass on the way in. The cove itself is small and secluded, with a white crescent beach which ends at a rocky section of tidepools and large sea caves. It is a good place for swimming, crabbing, diving for scallops, or just fish-watching. When the tide is low, you can stand on the tidepool shelf and watch a colorful array of tropical fish in the underwater gardens.

You can sometimes buy fish or shellfish at Rancho Juncalito, a fish camp 6 miles south of Nopoló. On the beach you'll see the salted meat of *tiburón* (shark) hung on lines to dry, a familiar sight at similar camps on the Baja coasts. Salted *tiburón* is sold all over Mexico as *bacalao*, though this word actually means "salt cod."

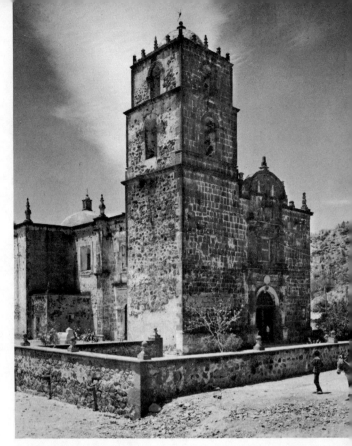

SAN JAVIER'S impressive mission is village gathering place. Old burial crypts fill courtyard, left.

About 3 miles south of Juncalito is the turn to Puerto Escondido, the shipping port for the agricultural produce of the Santo Domingo valley. There are grand plans for the development of Escondido, but at present it consists of only a pier. If you stop to fish-watch, you may be hooked for hours. The shore drops off sharply here, and when the early morning rays of the sun penetrate the water you see a technicolor parade of fish go by.

There are several camping spots on the stony shore south of Escondido. The beaches are strewn with turtle shells and washed-up pufferfish, the spiny souvenirs sold by vendors in La Paz.

Leaving the Sea of Cortez, the road winds up a mountain and then straightens out and traverses a flat, dusty desert to Villa Insurgentes, a distance of 58 miles from Escondido.

The Comondús

The two Comondús, San Miguel and San José, lie near the end of the vast lava plateau that extends southeast from San Ignacio. Nestling in a deep, sheer-walled canyon, these villages are among the most attractive oases on the peninsula. The narrow canyon road is a path through a jungle of sugar

SILVERY OLIVE TREES shade the peaceful plaza of San José Comondú. Tourists are rarely seen in the twin Comondús, once on the main highway but now bypassed by the new Gulf road.

cane, mangoes, papayas, and other fruits. In this fertile valley everything grows to enormous size. The lemons of Comondú, the villagers say, are as large as a man's head.

San Miguel has a toy of a church, a small brick chapel whose blue and white tower, despite its size, stands above the village and surrounding valley. The original mission church of San José is gone, but one of the old mission buildings is now being used as a church.

It is the plaza of San José, however, that has the most appeal. Shaded by four 60-year-old olive trees, it is a cool and serene place to escape the midday heat. Behind a crumbling adobe wall beyond the plaza is a garden of fruit trees dwarfed by a gnarled old olive.

Originally on the main highway to La Paz, the two Comondús are now bypassed by the new road. Few visitors reach these remote villages anymore. There are no accommodations or restaurants for travelers, but if you needed a place to stay overnight, you could probably find a hospitable home. Even to buy soft drinks you have to go to a private residence.

Although there are several ways to reach the Comondús, the best road is from Villa Insurgentes. It is a good dirt road and easy to drive, but very dusty. Along the way in the vicinity of Santo Domingo and Pozo Grande grows one of the strangest of Baja's strange cacti—the creeping devil cactus (*Machaerocereus eruca*), which sprawls on the ground and looks like a mass of spiny caterpillars.

The La Paz highway

The Gulf route joins the paved La Paz highway at Villa Insurgentes—150 miles from La Paz. This is a booming agricultural area. Villa Insurgentes, with its broad, shop-lined boulevard, has the flavor of an American farm town. The cultivated acres that extend for miles resemble the Midwest.

After the last farm is passed, the highway crosses the long, flat Magdalena Desert. *Cardones* and tree yuccas dominate the landscape. To the west is Magdalena Bay, the largest natural bay on the continent, where a series of sheltered estuaries and lagoons extends for 150 miles. Migrating gray whales come to the lagoons in winter to bear young.

Nearing La Paz, there is a noticeable change in climate as you leave the cooling influence of the Pacific and approach the tropics. At the top of a high hill about 20 miles from La Paz you have your first glimpse of the "pearl of the peninsula."

Southward to

the Cape

The modern city of La Paz and the peninsula's tropical tip...quiet little villages and luxurious resorts

SANDY SHORES washed by a tropical sea beckon the beachcomber on the South Cape. Tidepools near Japanese shipwreck harbor exotic fish.

MUCH OF what is distinctive about Lower California can be found in its Cape region, which extends from La Paz to land's end at Cabo San Lucas. From modern La Paz you can journey in one or two hour's time into another era where people live simply in palm-thatched houses, *vaqueros* ride on saddles little changed from Spanish colonial days, and sugar cane is made into panocha exactly as it was a century ago. In the interior lies a mountain range as wild and unexplored as any place on the peninsula, with Shangri-las hidden away in remote canyons that can be reached only by horse or mule.

Many of the more unusual desert plants from farther north grow in the Cape region—*cardones*, grotesque *torote* trees, sweet and sour pitahayas —in some places in tangles so thick and impenetrable they form a desert jungle. Others are found nowhere else in Baja—the *cardón barbón*, a smaller, more bristly species of *cardón*; a diminutive sweet pitahaya with cherry-sized fruit; and a lavender-flowered hedgehog cactus.

The tropical waters of the Cape region literally teem with game fish—and this is the only place where you can fish for marlin the year around. Modern fishing resorts, each with its own airstrip, are strategically located near the best fishing grounds and can be reached by light plane from the border in five or six hours. The simplest resort is comparable to a good motel in the United States. The most lavish offers such luxuries as onyx baths, carved stone idols for barstools, and prime steaks flown in from the States.

Once remote and difficult to reach, the Cape region is now only two hours by jet from Los Angeles. By automobile, it is an overnight ferry trip from the Mexican mainland. Recent improvements in the 248-mile loop road, including paving of more than half, theoretically make it possible to drive around the entire Cape region in one or two days. However, to see something of the life in the little tropical villages you have to allow plenty of time to make contacts with the people who live in them. This can be the richest part of the traveling experience. If you don't speak at least a little Spanish, try to take along someone who does. Perhaps you can arrange through the manager of one of the fishing resorts to borrow one of his staff as interpreter and guide for a day.

YOUNG VENDOR shaves ice for refreshing fruit raspadas, eaten like ice cream cones. These are just one of the kinds of treats sold on the streets of downtown La Paz.

The Cape region offers good weather and interesting things to do almost any month of the year. Summer heat can be oppressive, but summer is the season when billfishing is at its best—and also when many of the most delicious tropical fruits ripen. The desert is greenest in autumn, after the summer rains, and desert flowers are in bloom. Thousands of ducks spend part of the winter in fresh-water lagoons on the Gulf, and inland valleys are filled with dove and quail. In spring, the sugar cane is harvested and made into candy, and the desert has another flowering season when the *cardones*, mesquites, and palo verdes burst into bloom.

LA PAZ

Not long ago La Paz was a sleepy little fishing port with a pearl industry that was largely a memory. The discovery of the big-game fishing potential in cape waters, however, has brought a surge of life to Baja Sur's capital city. La Paz is finding a place as a tourist center for the Cape region and as a sport-fishing center.

The changes are evident everywhere, in the modern city buildings and the recently paved streets. Along the *malecón*, the beautiful waterfront drive shaded with laurels and clusters of coconut palms, shops and tourist services are sprouting. There is a place that specializes in scuba-diving gear, another that rents four-wheel-drive vehicles for exploring the skin-diving coves and swimming beaches beyond town. There are offices ready to sign you up for a sport-fishing excursion beyond La Paz Bay or to make your reservation at a fishing resort. New curio stores sell foreign imports and Mexican craftwork, and restaurants specialize in the area's bountiful seafood. At La Perla's sidewalk restaurant, where you can linger over coffee and watch the ever-changing harbor traffic or one of the fiery sunsets for which La Paz is renowned, the tables are often thronged, particularly on weekends.

Back from the *malecón*, the old La Paz provides sharp contrasts with the new. In the downtown district the picturesque maze of crooked streets, some cobblestoned, is congested with traffic in morning and late afternoon. *Supermercados*, styled after United States supermarkets (and as well stocked), are but a few blocks from open-air stands overflowing with foods in colorful profusion. The graceful old windmills, long the highest landmarks of La Paz, now compete for skyline space with television antennas atop modern homes. At the ultra-modern jetport, the grass is cut by hand shears; elsewhere, you may see goats doing the job. Broad paved avenues lead to the modern Governor's Palace on Avenida Isabela la Catolica, but a few blocks farther the dusty streets end in the desert.

All the changes give La Paz an air of excitement. But it is still a city of grace and charm. Walk along the quiet residential streets and you see bright bougainvillea spilling over brick walls, gardens filled with figs and plums, and showy *arboles del fuego*, or flame trees, with long brown pods and masses of burnt-orange blossoms. For a different picture of La Paz, in its matchless setting on a sweep of bay, drive a few miles southwest of town to the palm-lined beach that curves around the inner harbor. At dawn the city looks golden in the distance. At night its lights glitter like diamonds strung along the waterfront.

Although many people in La Paz are bilingual, English is not generally spoken in banks, the post office, or the telephone company. If you need an interpreter, go to the Department of Tourism, on the second floor of the Governor's Palace on Avenida Isabela la Catolica. Someone there will make telephone calls and inquiries for you.

Shopping

Most of the gift shops, department stores, and specialty boutiques are strung along the *malecón* or clustered in a few blocks in the downtown business district. You can buy good craftwork from all over Mexico (including hand-embroidered dresses from Guadalajara) in Artesania Mexicana on the *malecón*, in several curio stores just around the block, and in the hotel gift shops. Other stores sell imported articles—French perfumes, for instance. Local specialties are gifts from the sea—dried spiny pufferfish, varnished green-turtle shells, and even the translucent pearls that once made La Paz world-famous.

Browse in La Perla de la Paz, a maze of shops selling almost everything you can think of. La Perla is also a money exchange where, with the proper identification and photographs, checks and money orders can be cashed—even in afternoons and on holidays when regular banks are closed.

During the morning hours, the shopping area below Avenida Revolución and bordered by Independencia and 16 de Septiembre is the liveliest place in town. In between the tiny specialty shops and the *zapaterías* (shoe stores) crowded with sandals are stores selling everyday wares. Here you'll find the real, untouristy life of La Paz. In a dark, cavernous central market, a heady array of fruits, vegetables, pungent chiles, and hunks of meat are displayed, along with such items as straw hats, sandals, guitars, bolts of cloth, Mexican comic books, and religious artifacts. In the street, vendors sell refreshing *raspadas* (shaved ice flavored with the syrup of your choice), *dulces calabazas* (candied squash rind), and even *hamburguesas*.

You might as well forget trying to buy anything (or find anyone) between the hours of 11 a.m. and 3 p.m. Nearly everyone retreats to the shade for the midday siesta, and the shops, banks, and businesses pull down their blinds. Along the *malecón* beach people sleep or snack in the shade of the palm-thatched "toadstool" sun shades. You may see feet dangling from the laurel trees, as someone stays cool in the greenery of the branches. Gay *sombrillas*, or parasols, appear on the street, and ingenious headshades are devised, such as an empty cornflakes carton atop a little boy's head. In the late afternoon, when the southerly breeze begins to blow, the shops and streets of the city come alive again.

Where to eat

La Paz offers more choices for dining out than any other place in the southern peninsula. The fare is less than epicurean, but the atmosphere, complete with strolling mariachis, couldn't be pleasanter. Candlelit hotel dining rooms exude Spanish colonial charm and hospitality; open-air restaurants with palm-thatched dining nooks have a South Seas flavor. Along the *malecón* are restaurants with harbor views or flower-filled patios.

The best eating is in the large resort hotels and in several restaurants scattered throughout the city. Hotel fare tends to cater to north-of-the-border tastes, though all hotels serve Mexican specialties and some set aside a night each week for a Mexican buffet. Restaurants such as El Serape and Los Candiles (in the downtown shopping district) and Voltic and Cuatro Vientos (near the airport) offer interesting menus of Mexican dishes, infinitely more varied than the tacos, tamales, and enchiladas that some tourists think comprise the range of Mexican cuisine.

There are several places that feature charcoal-broiled steaks and meats, including Las Brisas on the *malecón*. But the fresh catch of the shrimpers and fishermen provides the finest food in La Paz. Stroll along the *malecón* and stop in at Laury's for a piquant cocktail of the succulent Baja butter clams or a bowl of *sopa de mariscos*, a spicy seafood soup of shrimps, clams, cabrilla, and red snapper—or whatever the cook happened to pick out at the fish market. Any place you find it, try a *seviche* of the flavorful scallops divers get from Gulf waters. The great specialty of Baja, the *caguama* (green turtle), is most frequently encountered as breaded and fried turtle "steaks"—the way most tourists like their turtle. But there is an occasional turtle barbecue (at La Posada, for example), turtle soup (offered weekly at Los Arcos in turtle season), and, with advance notice, stuffed turtle fins (at

Cuatro Vientos), an offbeat specialty for the adventurous diner.

Hotels will sometimes prepare turtle barbecues and Mexican clambakes for a group upon request. You can also look up Angel Verdugo, a taxi driver whose sideline is a steamed-clam picnic on the clamming beach about 15 miles west of town. A day's outing generally lasts from about 10 a.m. to 3 p.m. You help dig the clams by feeling them with your toes. The cost for the clam feast is about $40 for five persons, $28 for two. Angel can be located at the taxi stand in front of the Hotel Continental.

Arts and antiquities

You can watch young potters at work at the Center of Regional Arts, the first arts and crafts school in Baja. Both a school and a workshop, the Center was founded in 1966 and now supports itself by

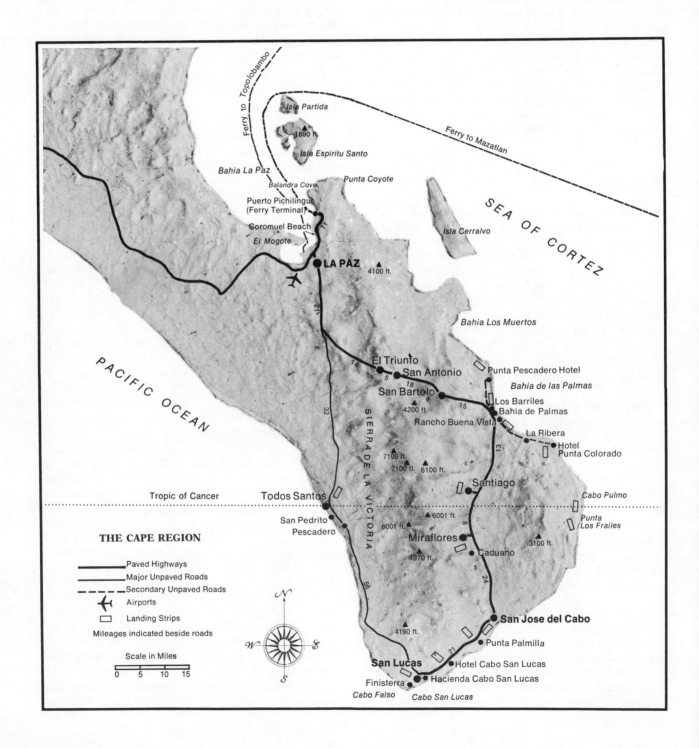

THE CAPE REGION

— Paved Highways
— Major Unpaved Roads
--- Secondary Unpaved Roads
✈ Airports
▭ Landing Strips
Mileages indicated beside roads

Scale in Miles
0   5   10   15

sales of its ceramic ware and craftwork. Girls weave palm fronds into baskets, design and make dresses, and fashion winsome animal toys from colorful remnants. A wide variety of the craftwork and glazed ware (including vases, mugs, and multi-colored pottery necklaces) is sold in a room next to the potters' workshop. The potters generally work from 9 a.m. to 2 p.m., but the shop stays open later in the afternoon. The Center's work is also sold in several gift shops and grocery stores in town.

The Center is on Legaspy, past the Governor's Palace (a sign on Avenida Isabela la Catolica points the direction). Another shop, devoted primarily to handmade dresses, is on the main highway just south of town.

The Museo Antropológico de La Paz is next to the library west of the plaza. The museum is in its infancy, but eventually it is hoped it will house many exhibits devoted to the early history of Baja. Of special interest now is a skeleton of a Pericu (one of the original Indian tribes of the Cape region) discovered near San José del Cabo.

Beaches

The best swimming close to La Paz is at Coromuel Beach, 2½ miles north of the *malecón* toward the Pichilingue ferry terminal. (Swimming in the city's inner bay is not advisable.) Coromuel is a small crescent beach backed by a *cardón*-covered hill. On a sunny day, the water here is intensely blue, the sand a blinding white. You can picnic in the shade of the palm-thatched toadstools that line the beach or in a roofed patio on a bluff. A refreshment stand offers tacos, sandwiches, soft drinks, and ice cream. On holidays and weekends Coromuel is popular with sunbathers, waterskiers, and families on outings. On weekdays you can have it almost completely to yourself.

Farther along on the ferry road are several sandy, mangrove-bordered coves and long stretches of beach. A favorite destination for skin-divers and swimmers is exquisite Balandra Cove. It lies beyond the ferry terminal at Bahía Pichilingue, but the dirt road that leads to it turns off before the ferry terminal. Balandra is difficult to find; ask for precise directions in town.

Fishing and cruises

In season there is fishing for marlin (mid-March to mid-October) and sailfish (May to December) in the Gulf. The sport-fishing boats ($50 to $60 a day) leave from two piers: the public pier in the center of town and the pier at Hotel Continental.

Fishing in the bay is excellent. Varieties caught include fighting roosterfish, corvina, dolphinfish, bonefish, snook, sierra, grouper, yellowtail, and many others. It is advisable to bring your own tackle for bay fishing.

Ten-day houseboat excursions into the Sea of Cortez aboard the 121-foot *Marisla II* originate at La Paz and continue up the coast as far as Loreto, with stops for fishing, exploring, beachcombing, and diving at islands. Rates are $450 per cruise per person. For information write to La Paz Skin Diving Service, Box 133, La Paz, B.C.

YOU CAN WATCH potters and weavers at work at Center of Regional Art. Handicrafts are for sale.

Where to stay

Six hotels in La Paz, some with swimming pools and full resort facilities, cater to tourists. The two oldest are Hotel Perla, a large commercial hotel, and Hotel Los Arcos, both on Avenida Alvaro Obregón on the waterfront. La Posada and Hotel Continental (formerly Hotel Los Cocos) are both situated on the beach on adjoining properties 2 miles south of town. Hotel Guaycura and Hotel Calafia, also 2 miles south of town, are on opposite sides of the main highway. All offer accommodations and meals on the American plan. Rates range from $20 to $36 for two, with Los Arcos, Continental, and La Posada at the upper end of the range. La Perla has inexpensive European plan accommodations. La Paz also has several less luxurious hotels with lower rates.

Two motels offer minimal overnight accommodations as well as hook-ups for trailers and space for tent camping. Motel El Cardon is 2½ miles south on the main highway leading into town. El Sombrerito, a half mile off the main highway (a sign marks the right turn as you come into town), has a palm-thatched ramada for shade at each site. Both places have hot-water showers.

Camping

Tent and trailer sites are available at the motels in town. Open camping is possible on the beaches north of La Paz (beyond the ferry terminal). South of the city along the inner bay, there are many miles of undeveloped beach terminating at the long, sandy peninsula called El Mogote. Wherever you can find a clearing in the cactus, you can camp on the desert along the main highway north of La Paz and south toward the Cape region. (Campers should note that white gas and fuels for camp stoves aren't available in La Paz. The only cooking fuel is aviation gas, which can be obtained at the airport.)

Transportation

Four commercial airlines—Aeronaves de Mexico, Aeronaves del Oeste, Aerolineas del Pacifico, and Air West—make regularly scheduled flights to La Paz (see page 6). In addition, Servicios Aereos Especiales provides an air-taxi service between La Paz and Rancho Las Cruces (a private club), Hotel Punta Pescadero, Hotel Bahía de Palmas, Rancho Buena Vista, Hotel Punta Colorada, Hotel Las Cruces Palmilla, Hotel Cabo San Lucas, and Hacienda Cabo San Lucas.

The ferries *Presidente Diaz Ordaz* and *La Paz*, owned and operated by the federal government,

BATHERS STAY COOL under palm-thatched umbrellas on beaches of La Paz. This is Coromuel.

each make two round trips a week across the Gulf of California between La Paz and Mazatlán. The ferries arrive and depart from the Pichilingue ferry terminal located 11 miles north of town. The 235-mile trip takes 17 hours one way. Schedules are posted on the window of the ferry office on Avenida Independencia in downtown La Paz. Rates for automobiles, based on vehicle length, range from $30 to $44. Passenger fares (per person) for the trip are $5.20 for reclining seats, $10 for rooms with four bunks, $24 to $48 for staterooms and suites.

The privately-owned ferry *Salvatierra* makes two round trips a week between La Paz and Topolobampo. The trip one way takes 10½ hours. Rates for automobiles range from $24 to $35.20. Passenger rates are $4.40 and $6. The terminal for the *Salvatierra* is about 1 mile south of town at Sonora Street.

Autotransportes Aguila operates bus service from La Paz to San José del Cabo with stops at San Bartolo, Los Barriles, and Buena Vista and a connecting station wagon from San José to Cabo San Lucas.

Taxis in La Paz charge hourly, daily, and trip rates. A one-way fare (up to five passengers) to Santiago or the East Cape resorts might be $25, to Hotel Cabo San Lucas about $50. The Hertz agency

COCONUT PALMS along the malecón *frame a sky streaked by one of La Paz's famous sunsets. Waterfront drive continues on to Coromuel Beach and the Pichilingue ferry terminal.*

in front of Hotel Perla rents automobiles, and Auto Rentas del Bremejo, with offices located on the *malecón* and at the airport, rents two and four-wheel-drive vehicles.

LA PAZ TO SAN JOSE DEL CABO

An excellent paved road extends to San José del Cabo and brings all the fishing resorts around Bahía de las Palmas within less than a two-hour's drive of La Paz. The highway cuts a wide path through flat, dusty desert, then climbs around hills to the villages of El Triunfo, San Antonio, and San Bartolo and makes the descent to the Gulf at the bay.

If you've driven through the deserts north of La Paz, you will notice some differences in the vegetation here. You will see more of the yellow-flowered *palo de arco*, which under favorable conditions grows to the size of a small tree. The *cardones* are stubbier than the stately giants that forest Baja's central desert. There are, in fact, two different species in the Cape region. One, known as *cardón pelón*, is "bald" (or nearly spineless) at the tops of the columnar branches. *Cardón barbón* is spinier; botanists call it *Pachycereus pecten-aboriginum*—

BANANA TRUCK is first to debark from the La Paz. *Ferry makes three round trips weekly to Mazatlan.*

"comb of the aborigines"—because the Indians used the tawny, bristle-covered fruits as combs for their hair.

A few miles north of Santiago the road crosses the Tropic of Cancer. The change is imperceptible at first, but as you journey farther south there is a heavy tropical feeling in the oases luxuriant with fruits, and the desert becomes what botanists call the "Cape thorn forest," in places so dense it seems more like a desert jungle. *Cardones*, sharp-spined chollas, and sour pitahayas crowd one another for space, forming barbed barriers impenetrable to all but such desert inhabitants as jackrabbits, birds, and kangaroo rats.

In years when summer rains send torrents of water through parched arroyos, the coral vine *(Antigonon leptopus)* winds through the washes and climbs over the *cardones*, covering them with a blaze of red flowers. *Torote* trees and plants that were gaunt skeletons develop green leaves along their branches.

An aromatic, yellow-flowered shrub known as damiana turns up in the Cape region. It is esteemed for its supposed aphrodisiac properties. The dried leaves are diffused for a restorative tea and also made into a liqueur that flavors the Margaritas served at Cape resorts.

El Triunfo and San Antonio

Twin spires of a bright little church and the tall stack of a smelter afford the traveler his first view of the ghost mining town of El Triunfo, about 35 miles from La Paz. Walk around the still streets and you find that some of the town's inhabitants are burros who occupy the crumbling adobes and wander from one building to another like townspeople visiting their neighbors. At the now-defunct silver mine, which dates back to 1862 and employed many thousands in its prosperous years, you may be approached by a grizzled old miner toting a bucket of heavy nuggets that look, and feel, like pure lead and silver— he sells the nuggets as souvenirs of the old mine.

On the highway past the church is a thatched-roof stand displaying craftwork made of palm—a native material offering more promise than the silver-laden ore. Some of the work is very attractive, and the prices are reasonable. About half a dozen girls in town weave the palm fronds into pocketbooks, baskets, and flat trays.

About 5 miles south is San Antonio, another settlement with a silver-mining past. You must make a short detour from the highway (turn right); otherwise you could drive by the town without even seeing it. Interest in the silver of San Antonio began in 1756. The mines were worked

sporadically and flourished briefly until mining activities began to be centered in El Triunfo instead of San Antonio.

San Antonio is a pretty little town of old adobe buildings and tall, skirtless palms. The handsome church on the village plaza, built in 1825 and remodeled since then, is distinguished for its simplicity and dignity.

San Bartolo

Situated in a narrow, spring-fed canyon about 18 miles beyond San Antonio, San Bartolo is one of the greenest and most colorful villages in the southern peninsula. Palm-thatched *jacales*, bright with bougainvillea, cling to the terraced slopes of the canyon. In early summer, the sweet smell of ripening fruits is everywhere. Trees droop under their loads of mangoes, figs, guavas, and bananas. Citrus and avocados abound, as do fields of sugar cane. (In spring, when the crop is harvested, the local children eat the cane like candy, stripping it with their teeth.) Some of the gardens around homes in the village have glossy-leaved coffee trees; when the berries turn red they are picked and roasted.

PALM BASKET tempts traveler at El Triunfo. Local palm craftwork is sold at roadside stand.

Along the rock areas of the arroyo grow some of the most magnificent *zalates*, or wild fig trees, on the peninsula—massive, spreading trees with networks of white roots that crawl over, in, and around boulders.

The main highway passes by a restaurant, a few dwellings, and a couple of grocery stores, but most of San Bartolo lies downhill in the arroyo. In season, the grocery stores sell locally made fruit preserves, such as guava paste and *conserva de naranja*, a thick, syrupy conserve made with orange peel and panocha. In San Bartolo, as in many towns in Baja, fresh empanadas or tamales are sold door to door.

The East Cape resorts

The largest concentration of fishing resorts south of La Paz is in the East Cape area of the Gulf coast between Punta Pescadero and Punta Colorada. These resorts are more informal and less expensive ($28 to $32 a day double, with meals) than those lining the tip of the peninsula, and they offer comfortable cottages or motel-type cottage clusters. All share superb year-round big-game fishing. A unique combination of conditions attracts marlin and sail-

fish, dolphinfish, yellowtail, tuna, and roosterfish to this particular part of the Sea of Cortez. Many record catches have come from here, including a 1,056-pound marlin. There is also good fishing from shore for *pargo* (red snapper), sierra, and bonito. Rates for cruisers range from $55 to $70 a day. Typical rates for skiffs are $25 a day; $5 for tackle.

To reach the area from La Paz by land taxi costs about $25, by air taxi about $15 a seat. All the resorts can be reached by short-wave radio through Servicios Aereos, the air-taxi service at the La Paz airport. Both Rancho Buena Vista and Hotel Bahía de Palmas can be reached through representatives in La Paz.

Northernmost of the group of resorts is Hotel Punta Pescadero, reached from Los Barriles by a 9-mile narrow shelf road that winds along the coastal cliffs. The hotel is perched on a steep bluff above the beach, and every room has an osprey's-eye view of the Gulf. Indian burial caves have been found both north and south of the hotel, as have petroglyphs, projectile points, and a spear-thrower now in the museum of the University of Mexico. The whole area, rich in Indian remains, is largely unexplored. Hotel Punta Pescadero has its own airstrip.

The largest of the resorts is Rancho Buena Vista.

BURROS WANDER in and out of abandoned adobes in El Triunfo, an old silver-mining community. You can explore the ruins of the inactive smelter, whose smokestack towers above town.

The Cape 71

THE BAJA VAQUERO

The cowboy tradition, fast becoming part of the American past, is still very much alive in Lower California. The Baja *vaquero* leads a hard life, living in the brush for weeks or months at a time. He sleeps on the ground, using a leather sleeping bag and his saddle for a pillow. In cold weather a small fire is kept burning through the night.

The leather garments worn by the *vaquero* are designed for protection from the sharp spines and thorns of the densely vegetated desert in the Cape region. This clothing is essentially the same as that worn 200 years ago when Spaniards colonized the peninsula, and the saddle is basically the Spanish colonial saddle.

The Santiago *vaquero* (shown in the photograph) wears the traditional leather *sombrero vaqueteado*. The brim of the hat is woven of palm leaves and covered with deerskin. The wraparound knee-length coat, also of deerskin, is called the *cuera*. Protecting the legs are calfskin *armas*, leather skirts that are the forerunners of chaps.

A *cojinillo*, with two large pockets in front protected by overlapping flaps, covers the saddle. The *reata*, a rawhide rope, is coiled around a pocket of the *cojinillo*.

Meals are served family-style at long tables, and guests are summoned to dinner by the blowing of a conch shell. The ranch raises its own vegetables, fruits, cattle, and pigs and has a large smokehouse where the guests' catches can be cured. Children can go for burro rides. There is a private airstrip.

A mile north of Buena Vista in the village of Los Barriles is Hotel Bahía de Palmas, a quieter and smaller resort. It is set in attractive surroundings of palm trees on the beautiful sandy beach that borders the bay; an airstrip is next to the hotel.

Hotel Punta Colorada, 15 miles south of Buena Vista between Puntas Colorada and Arena, is the newest and most isolated of these coastal resorts. The hotel is reached by a sandy road that winds through the thick desert scrub beyond La Ribera, where fresh-water lagoons harbor thousands of migrating ducks in the winter months. The hotel has its own airstrip.

Santiago

You could drive into Santiago, look around the sleepy plaza surrounded by adobe stores and buildings and a single gas pump, and be on your way again without realizing that you're in one of the principal agricultural and cattle-raising areas south of La Paz. Santiago doesn't advertise its attractions, and the casual traveler is likely to miss them.

The irrigated valleys around the town are green in early spring with sugar cane and fruit trees. An old sugar mill *(trapiche)* crushes the cane and makes it into the brown-sugar cones of panocha loved all over Mexico.

Horse races—one of the major events in Baja Sur—are held here every year in July to celebrate Santiago's day. The horses, trained secretly, come from all over the southern peninsula. Young boys, using no saddles, are the jockeys. During the three-day fiesta there is heavy betting. Many orchestras play for dances, and there are strolling mariachis. All kinds of food and wares are sold in outdoor markets.

The Santiago valley is the southern peninsula's center for white-winged dove and quail hunting. The season usually extends from November through March. Expeditions into the mountains are also made for hunting mountain lion and deer.

SKIFF brings in catch from sport-fishing boats at Rancho Buena Vista, one of East Cape resorts.

FINE LEATHERWORK is specialty of a few crafts-men in Miraflores. Chair like this is made to order.

Arrangements for hunting and pack trips into the mountains can be made at the Hotel Palomar. (All you need for a hunting permit is $19.20 and a photograph. These are mailed to La Paz, and the license is returned in three or four days. You also can obtain a permit directly in La Paz.) The Palomar, an attractive hotel with rooms around a secluded courtyard ($20 for two, American plan), is set amid papayas, bananas, and many flowering trees, including the *Bauhinia,* or "orchid tree," with showy lavender blossoms. The Palomar's guests are served authentic Mexican dishes—such as *menudo, machaca, chiles rellenos,* and *carne asada.*

Miraflores

Miraflores, the leather-working center of the southern peninsula, is a pleasant little village of sun-baked adobes and wide, tree-shaded dirt streets, about 8 miles past Santiago. Many of the leather garments that are the distinctive garb of the Baja *vaquero* are made here and in the neighboring village of Caduaño. The leather craftsmen also make

the intricately tooled saddles *vaqueros* use, as well as belts, sandals, sport-fishing vests, and wrought-iron chairs with leather backs and seats. Most products are made to order. A chair, for example, takes about a month. But occasionally there are a few readymade items, such as sandals and minia-ture saddles, which can be purchased from the maker directly or in the general store in Miraflores. A well-known leather shop is Juan Castro Ceseña's.

Sierra de la Victoria

The Sierra de la Victoria, whose highest peaks are more than 7,000 feet high, extend nearly the length of the Cape region. The mountain slopes are for-ested with oak, madrone, hardwood *chino* and *guérivo,* and, at higher elevations, piñon pine. Deer browse in meadows, and mountain lions are found in remoter areas. Deep in the interior are streams, waterfalls, and isolated settlements, a day's trip by mule from the desert valley villages.

Cañon de la Zorra is one of several mountain hideaways in the region. In 1968 two San Diego newspapermen made a pack trip to the canyon and

BUZZARDS watch and wait from cardon, a favorite roost. Scavenger on left is the uncommon caracara.

visited a family of French ancestry who had settled there in 1913 amid a paradise of semitropical fruits, growing citrus, papayas, avocados, and even their own coffee and tea.

No roads, not even primitive tracks, lead into the Victoria range. To reach the mountains you need guides, horses, and mules. Special arrangements must be made for pack trips. Inquire at the villages of Santiago or Todos Santos or at one of the Cape's fishing resorts.

San José del Cabo

Narrow, winding, hilly streets bordered with brightly-painted houses lead to the shady plaza of San José, the largest town south of La Paz. On one corner of the plaza a refreshment stand sells snacks and cold drinks under a canopy that provides welcome relief from the sun. Behind it is a new municipal building, its modern façade a startling contrast to the weathered old adobes you see nearby.

Dominating the plaza is the town's new church, built in the 1940's. A colored mural above the entrance depicts the rebellion of 1734, when all the missions from La Paz south were wiped out in an Indian uprising.

East of town lies a fine, wide sandy beach where the swimming is good and the surf fishing even better. At a shark-fishing camp on the beach, salted hunks of shark meat are hung over lines like laundry drying in the sun. The drive to the beach through a green and lovely area takes you past rich, well-watered farmland where sugar cane, corn, and many vegetables and orchard fruits grow. The great mango trees that line the dirt road bear some of the sweetest-tasting mangoes you'll find anywhere in Baja.

Casa O'Fisher, a small hotel in town with an adjoining restaurant, is under new management. Señora O'Fisher, remembered by many travelers for her good cooking, moved from San José to Cabo San Lucas several years ago.

THE SOUTH CAPE

The scenic 21-mile stretch from San José to Cabo San Lucas winds around headlands above the sea, dips into arroyos, and passes many secluded coves lined with sparkling white beaches. Brown pelicans preen on guano-whitened rocks close to shore, and cormorants at rest dry their outspread wings. Sometimes as many as a hundred pelicans are seen, but their numbers are declining.

All along the road vultures are seen clustering around beach wrack, picking clean the bones of discarded fish. At dusk they roost atop *cardones* or on the twisted branches of *torote* trees. Occasionally you see in their midst the much rarer desert scavenger, the striking crested caracara, a long-legged black and white bird with a scarlet face. In the rock piles by the roadside, lizards (including desert iguanas) bask in the sun.

To explore this fascinating coast, take the old road wherever you can. It follows closer to the shore than the new road, sometimes leading to a beach or cove, sometimes turning inland to go over or around a rocky point or headland, sometimes

AT HOTEL CABO SAN LUCAS swimmers have choice of pool or waters of Puerto Chileno Bay.

NATURAL SEA ARCH marks bottom of Baja, where Pacific and Gulf waters meet. Boats can be rented for a close-up view.

IN MOORISH SPLENDOR, luxurious Hotel Palmilla sits on rocky promontory of South Cape. Tiled swimming pool through arch overlooks sea.

disappearing altogether where the new road bull-dozed it out of existence. Several accesses to the beach and to good camping spots can be found from the old road—particularly along the stretch between Hotel Cabo San Lucas and the town of Cabo San Lucas.

About 3 miles beyond Hotel Cabo San Lucas is the wreck of a Japanese ship that ran aground in 1966. Near the wreck are tidepools filled with purple sea urchins, sea anemones, brittle stars, and tiny multistriped fish. Not far down the beach, rock pinnacles carved into bizarre shapes by the surf protrude through the sand like jagged stalagmites. At the bottom of a few rocks are small basins where the retreating tides have left deposits of pure salt.

All along this coast there are coves lined with sandy beaches where you can swim and skin-dive in tropical waters with temperatures in the mid-seventies.

Luxury resorts

About 5 miles from San José you reach the first of several palatial fly-in resorts. In the sheltered coves where these resorts now anchor their marlin fleets, English privateers once hid while waiting to plunder the richly laden Manila galleons bringing Oriental silks and spices to Acapulco.

Commanding the edge of a cliff at the top of a long headland, Hotel Las Cruces Palmilla stands out brightly against the deep blue water, its white stucco walls, Spanish red tile roof, and mission-style campanile gleaming in the tropic sun. Colorful ceramic tiles and iron grillwork evoke the quiet elegance of an earlier era. The fountain in the center of the serene courtyard seems to have the patina of age, almost as though its stones had been cut and put in place by early padres. Rates are $56 a day for two, American plan. Sport-fishing cruisers are $60 to $85 a day. There is an airstrip.

THE SEA was the sculptor of these monoliths on the beach behind Cabo San Lucas. The smooth, water-worn rocks seem to change their shapes as shadows shift and deepen.

Hotel Cabo San Lucas, in a splendid setting of sea, tidepools, and sandy beaches, sits on a rocky promontory overlooking Puerto Chileno Bay. With its lavish use of stone, its onyx baths, and a swimming pool fed by a waterfall, this is the most luxurious fishing resort on the Baja California peninsula. Rates are $40 to $60 a day for two, American plan. Sport-fishing cruisers are about $74 a day. There is an airstrip.

The charming Hacienda Cabo San Lucas fronts on the sandy shores of San Lucas Bay in the small village of Cabo San Lucas. The hotel's Spanish-style architecture is a blend of old mission days and modern beach resort. Rates start at about $40 a day for two, and sport-fishing boats are $50 a day. An airstrip is located directly in back of the fishing resort. The hotel recently changed ownership, and the name is to be changed to Camino Real Cabo San Lucas.

In 1970 construction began on two new resorts in

Cabo San Lucas—Finisterra (on a cliff between Cabo San Lucas and Cabo Falso) and Bajo Colorado.

Cabo San Lucas

At Cabo San Lucas, the road turns inland and the peninsula seems to come to a dramatic end with a jagged ridge of granite cliffs extending a mile into the ocean. (Baja's southernmost point actually comes several miles beyond.) This is where the currents of the Gulf and Pacific waters meet. A great natural sea arch, visible for miles, marks the end of the ridge. Beyond it the waves surge around the two jagged pinnacles known as *Los Frailes* (the Friars), the tallest rising 291 feet above the water. The underwater shelf drops off steeply near here, forming an extensive submarine canyon where sand flows down the granite walls like waterfalls and exotic fish swim in colorful marine gardens of gorgonion coral.

You can rent a motorboat and guide (the price is negotiable) at the tuna-cannery pier or the Hacienda Cabo San Lucas for a close look at the arch and the small colony of sea lions that often can be seen on the seaweed-covered ledges at the base of one of the Friars. Or you can hire someone to row you out in a skiff. Local boatmen make sport of running through the sea arch. Another favorite pastime at Cabo San Lucas is to stand on the tuna cannery's long pier and watch the incredible numbers of large fish that feed on the tuna wastes.

Around the tip of the Cape, a beautiful sandy beach is backed by rocks sculptured into weird, surrealistic shapes. The beach is reached by a narrow road that runs out as far as the granite quarry. Close to shore, an old sunken wreck lies in about 50 feet of water.

A very long airfield serving the area lies 4 miles north of town.

CABO SAN LUCAS TO LA PAZ

The western route from Cabo San Lucas back up to La Paz is a dirt road that joins the paved highway about 21 miles south of La Paz. The road makes a gradual ascent (with occasional rough spots) into the mountains, and from the summit you look down over low-lying hills to the distant dark waters of the Pacific—a memorable view when the sky is reddened by the setting sun. The slopes of the hills are covered with a rich tangle of *cardones*, pitahayas, grotesque *torote* trees, and silvery-barked palo blanco trees. In the haze of an early-morning fog, the desert plants have a strange, spectral beauty.

If you camp in the area during the warmer

ITINERANT POTTERY VENDOR fills his truck with wares in Tlaquepaque, crosses over on ferry, and tours Cape villages. Children of Cabo San Lucas bargain for clay whistles and pots.

months, you will also discover a wealth of insect life. Lights attract swirls of moths, which, in turn, draw dozens of scorpions. They scurry over the ground picking up the moths and running over the toes of your shoes.

After descending the mountain grade, the road parallels the Pacific for about 35 miles to Todos Santos, along the way passing through many small farming villages that are lush with fruit-laden trees and field crops in early summer. At Pescadero, a monumental mango stands by the roadside, in season its branches sagging with thousands of mangoes. Many side roads lead to the beach—and to good beach campsites—where long, rolling breakers pound the shore. Two swimming beaches favored by local residents are San Pedrito and Los Cerritos, both a few miles south of Todos Santos.

Todos Santos

Surrounded by fields of sugar cane and graced by enormous mango trees, Todos Santos is a picturesque town. Its narrow streets are lined with substantial adobe buildings, and in the spring the town is ablaze with *palo de arco* and tropical

shrubs and flowers. Although Todos Santos is, technically, in the tropics, there is little of the oppressive summer sultriness that hangs over most of southern Baja. Much of the time a cool ocean breeze dispels the heat of the desert. The town's handsome whitewashed church, with hand-carved doors, was built in the 1840's and rebuilt after its destruction in the severe hurricane of 1941.

If you are in town during the sugar cane harvest (from about late February through most of May), you can watch panocha being made and taffy pulled at the *trapiche*, the sugar mill—and be treated to more candy than you could possibly eat. The panocha-making process is so fascinating, it would be worthwhile to time a trip just to be on hand for the sugar season. It is one of the outstanding sights in Baja.

The dusty 32-mile stretch from Todos Santos to the paved highway leading to La Paz is mostly flat, with a few short, steep dips. If it weren't for the distinctive plant cover by the roadside, you might think you were driving through the southern Arizona desert. Roadrunners dart in and out of the scrub, red cardinals flash in the mesquite trees, and cactus wrens sit in the thorny branches of pitahayas.

CANDYMAKING IN TODOS SANTOS

Making the brown sugar called panocha has changed very little since journalist-traveler J. Ross Browne described the factory at Todos Santos in the 1860's: "The cane is cut into pieces, pressed between two rollers, and the juice boiled to reduce to the necessary consistency. The panocha is made in molds or cups containing about a half a pound; when dry, it is packed in square baskets made of tough stubs, tied at the ends in the fashion of a bird crib."

The open-air candy mill here is roofed with loosely woven limbs of *palo de arco*, which provide shade but permit the steam of the boiling candy to escape. Visitors are free to walk around and watch all the candymaking processes. The freshly cut cane is unloaded from a cart pulled by three burros. After the stalks are stripped of leaves, they are fed into a crushing machine. The juice flows through a narrow trough into the first of a series of large open vats, fired from underneath by wood.

The clear juice of the first pressing is considered a treat, and you may be offered a glass. It is slightly sweet and very refreshing. As the juice runs into the next vat, debris is strained out, lime is added to the syrup, and the juice gets progressively thicker and more golden in color. The sweet steam rising from the vats all but obscures the men working behind them.

When the syrup reaches the final vat, it is a rich warm brown, and it is beaten back and forth with a paddle until it thickens to the proper consistency. The syrup is then scooped up in wooden buckets and poured on long, narrow rectangular wooden molds with circular or square depressions. Someone goes up the line of molds and spreads the hardening syrup so that it will flow evenly into all the openings.

When the panocha has hardened, the molds are hit with a couple of blows of a mallet and the cones of candy tumble into bins. They are packed in *palo de arco* baskets (shaped just like the bird cribs of Browne's description) lined with dried sugar-cane stalks.

For taffy, the syrup is cooked to a higher temperature. It is poured onto a smooth brick slab and allowed to cool for a few minutes. A taffy puller peels off a mass of the candy, hangs it on a hook attached to a post, and begins to pull it. Often, two men on opposite sides of a post will throw taffy at the same time, rhythmically heaving it back and forth as the deep brown mass elongates into a thick rope, takes on a light tawny color, and stiffens.

HOT SYRUP spread in molds will harden into panocha, a brown sugar used all over Mexico.

PULLING TAFFY takes muscle and skill. After stiffening, the ropes are gathered into a mass.

Index

SELECTED READING

More than 2,800 books, articles, and other material published about Baja California between 1535 and 1964 are listed in *Baja California Bibliography* (two volumes) by Ellen C. Barrett (Bennett & Marshall, Los Angeles). A catalogue listing more than 200 publications on Baja California is available free from the Arthur H. Clark Company, 1264 South Central Avenue, Glendale, California 91204.

The following list includes some of the publications most helpful for the traveler:

Automobile Club of Southern California. Road map of Baja California; *Guide to Baja California del Norte; Guide to Baja California del Sur.* 1969.

Cannon, Ray, and *Sunset* editors. *How to Fish the Pacific Coast.* Menlo Park, Calif., Lane Magazine and Book Co., 1967.

_____*The Sea of Cortez.* Menlo Park. Calif., Lane Magazine and Book Co., 1966.

Cross, Cliff. *Baja California, Mexico.* Box 301, North Palm Springs, Calif., 1970.

Gerhard, Peter, and Howard Gulick. *Lower California Guidebook.* Glendale, Calif., Arthur H. Clark Co., 1968.

Jaeger, Edmund C. *The North American Deserts.* Stanford, Calif., Stanford University Press, 1957.

Krutch, Joseph Wood. *The Forgotten Peninsula.* New York, William Morrow & Co., 1961.

Krutch, Joseph Wood, and Eliot Porter. *Baja California and the Geography of Hope.* San Francisco, Sierra Club, 1967.

Robinson, John. *Camping and Climbing in Baja.* Glendale, Calif., La Siesta Press, 1967.

Senterfitt, Arnold. *Airports of Baja California.* San Francisco, Miller Freeman Publications, 1969.

_____Map of Baja California. San Francisco, Miller Freeman Publications, 1970.